The Parables of Jesus

*A Personal Commentary and
Other Essays*

Andrew Schatkin

Copyright © 2018 by The Rowman & Littlefield Publishing Group, Inc.
4501 Forbes Boulevard
Suite 200
Lanham, Maryland 20706
Hamilton Acquisitions Department (301) 459-3366

Unit A, Whitacre Mews, 26-34 Stannary Street,
London SE11 4AB, United Kingdom

All rights reserved

British Library Cataloging in Publication Information Available

Library of Congress Control Number: 2018938142
ISBN 978-0-7618-6931-3 (paper : alk. paper)—ISBN 978-0-7618-6932-0 (electronic)

♾™ The paper used in this publication meets the minimum requirements of American National Standard for Information Sciences—Permanence of Paper for Printed Library Materials, ANSI Z39.48—1984

Table of Contents

Preface   v
Acknowledgments   vii

1. The Parable of the Sower   1
2. The Parable of the Patient Husbandman   5
3. The Parable of the Mustard Seed   7
4. The Parable of the Wicked Husbandmen   9
5. The Parable of the Budding Fig Tree   13
6. The Parable of the Doorkeeper   17
7. The Parable of Going Before the Judge   21
8. The Parable of the Two Houses   23
9. The Parable of the Children in the Market   25
10. The Parable of the Return of the Unclean Spirit   27
11. The Parable of the Tares Among the Wheat   29
12. The Parable of the Leaven   31
13. The Parable of the Treasure   33
14. The Parable of the Pearl   35
15. The Parable of the Seine-net   37
16. The Parable of the Lost Sheep   39
17. The Parable of the Unmerciful Servant   41
18. The Parable of the Good Employer   43
19. The Parable of the Two Sons   47
20. The Parable of the Great Supper   49
21. The Parable of the Guest Without a Wedding Garment   53
22. The Parable of the Burglar   55
23. The Parable of the Servant Entrusted with Supervision   57
24. The Parable of the Ten Virgins   61
25. The Parable of the Pounds and Talents   63

26.	The Parable of the Last Judgment	67
27.	The Parable of the Two Debtors	71
28.	The Parable of the Good Samaritan	75
29.	The Parable of the Friend Who Asked for Help	77
30.	The Parable of the Rich Fool	79
31.	The Parable of the Barren Fig Tree	81
32.	The Parable of the Closed Door	83
33.	The Parable of the Choice of Places at the Table	85
34.	The Parable of the Tower Builder and the King Contemplating a Campaign	87
35.	The Parable of the Lost Drachma	89
36.	The Parable of the Prodigal Son	91
37.	The Parable of the Unjust Steward	95
38.	The Parable of the Rich Man and Lazarus	97
39.	The Parable of the Servant's Reward	101
40.	The Parable of the Unjust Judge	103
41.	The Parable of the Pharisee and the Publican	105
	Appendix I: The Ten Commandments or The Decalogue	107
	Appendix II: The Sermon on the Mount	111
	Appendix III: Additional Reflections	115
	Select Bibliography	119
	Index of Biblical Citations	125

Preface

When I was a very young person, I was sent regularly by my mother and father to attend Sunday school in the local Methodist Church. Thus, from a very early age, I acquired a familiarity with the Bible stories, such as the creation story; the story of Adam and Eve and the garden of Eden; the first murder by Cain by his brother Abel; the flood, where Noah built his Ark; and, of course, the long list of patriarchs. I remember other stories in the Old Testament, such as the story of Job, King David, King Saul, and, in fact, I was compelled to memorize a number of the Psalms.

I also acquired a familiarity with the stories in the Gospels. These stories are stories of Jesus' life; his virgin birth as foretold; his youth spent with his father Joseph as a carpenter; and, finally, the narratives connected with his three year ministry. I can mention other stories such as the three wise men's coming to his birth; the presence of the shepherds who saw the star in the East; his speaking at the age of twelve in the temple; and the various miracles and healings that he performed during his life, culminating in his entrance into Jerusalem, his trial before Pilate, and his ultimate crucifixion and resurrection. I may say that I acquired a familiarity with the parables or stories Jesus told to point out the heavenly message by means of practical facts and advice. In other words, the purpose of the parables was to make people see what Jesus thought was the truth in, so to speak, down to earth terms.

There are parables in the Old Testament as well. For example, in 2nd Samuel 12:1-7, David coveted Bathsheba, the wife of Uriah, and in order to get her for himself, he arranged to have Uriah killed. Thereafter, Nathan came to David and told him a parable. The parable, related in 2nd Samuel 12, is as follows.

> And the Lord sent Nathan to David. He came to him and said to him, "There were two men in a certain city, the one rich and the other poor. The rich man had very many flocks and herds, but the poor man had nothing but one little ewe lamb which he had bought. And he brought it up, and it grew up with him and with his children; it used to eat of his morsel, and drink from his cup and lie in his bosom, and it was like a daughter to him. Now there came a traveler to the rich man, and he was unwilling to take one of his own flock or herd to prepare for the wayfarer who had come to him, but he took the poor man's lamb and prepared it for the man who had come to him." Then David's anger was greatly kindled against the man; and he said to Nathan, "As the Lord lives, the man who has done this deserves to die; and he shall restore the lamb fourfold because he did this thing and because he had no pity."

This is one of the earliest parable examples. Another famous parable is found in Isaiah 5:1-7. The method of parabolic teaching was a practical one, to make people see things based on the abstract through a practical and pragmatic story. Of course, two of the most famous parables of Jesus were the parable of the Prodigal Son and the Parable of the Good Samaritan.

This little book will present my views as to the understanding and interpretation of Jesus' parables. Although I am a gross amateur in understanding the words of Christ, nevertheless, it is my hope that in this slim book I can shed some light on these stories: their message and their meaning that Jesus was trying to make us understand in these practical stories. I am including in the appendix, here, a list of the Gospel parables, and in each chapter of this book, I will reprint the parable stories and give my impressions and thoughts as to the meaning of Christ's words for all generations. Included in this book as well are my comments and thoughts concerning the Decalogue or the Ten Commandments, found in Exodus 20:1-17, and my comments on the Sermon on the Mount, found in Matthew 5:1-11 and Luke 6:20-22. It is my sincere hope and desire that this little book will serve to bring before those who choose to read it the message, commandments, and warnings that may be found in these parables, in which Jesus points the way to the next world beyond this one.

Acknowledgments

The writing of a book such as this is time consuming and is, and was, a great challenge. Any book, however, is the result of the help and assistance of others, as well as of what one has learned in the course of one's life.

Firstly, I am greatly indebted to my parents, who insisted on my having a religious education in the Christian faith. From my parents, as well as my sisters, I have always been exposed to the essentials of the Christian faith and observed, in the lives of my parents and in the manner they conducted their lives, their commitment to Christ. Not a day went by that I did not see my mother reading the Bible, and not a Sunday passed that my family did not attend church and hear the Christian message. This book is a result of my life with my family and of the way they directed me to live in Christian belief.

I am also indebted to two particular books which assisted me and pointed me in the right direction in writing this book and in offering here my interpretation of these parables. The first book, entitled *The Parables of Jesus,* is by William Barclay published by John Knox Press in 1999, and the second book is entitled *The Parables of Jesus* by Joachim Jeremias published by SCM Press in a translation first published in English in 1954. These books greatly assisted me in acquiring a greater understanding and comprehension of these parables, and I cannot say how grateful I am for their pointing me and helping me to understand and interpret these parables.

I also am greatly indebted in having the opportunity to read and re-read the Bible and in particular the four Gospels, where these parables are related by Jesus. It is only in reading these Gospels and the parables themselves that we can understand these little stories, which point us, each time, from an earthly practical narrative to heaven. It is only in reading the biblical text that we can acquire some understanding of the depth of thought and intellectual profundity found in these stories. I have much to be grateful and thankful for in having the opportunity to read these stories and perhaps to understand them.

Finally, I am indebted to two of my assistants in my office, Fabian Leon and Jennie Abutu, who assisted me in the typing and editing of this book.

I conclude this acknowledgment with a conclusion that it is only in reading the word of God that we can come to an understanding of ourselves, of others, and of the mind of God.

All biblical translations are from the Revised Standard Version (RSV), published and annotated by Oxford University Press.

Chapter 1
The Parable of the Sower

Mark 4.1–9
Again he began to teach beside the sea. And a very large crowd gathered about him, so that he got into a boat and sat in it on the sea; and the whole crowd was beside the sea on the land. And he taught them many things in parables, and in his teaching he said to them: "Listen! A sower went out to sow. And as he sowed, some seed fell along the path, and the birds came and devoured it. Other seed fell on rocky ground, where it had not much soil, and immediately it sprang up, since it had no depth of soil; and when the sun rose it was scorched, and since it had no root it withered away. Other seed fell among thorns and the thorns grew up and choked it, and it yielded no grain. And other seeds fell into good soil and brought forth grain, growing up and increasing and yielding thirtyfold and sixtyfold and a hundredfold." And he said, "He who has ears to hear, let him hear."

Luke 8.4–15
And when a great crowd came together and people from town after town came to him, he said in a parable: "A sower went out to sow his seed; and as he sowed, some fell along the path and was trodden under foot, and the birds of the air devoured it. And some fell on the rock; and as it grew up, it withered away, because it had no moisture. And some fell among thorns; and the thorns grew with it and choked it. And some fell into good soil and grew and yielded a hundredfold." As he said this, he called out, "He who has ears to hear, let him hear." And when his disciples asked him what this parable meant, he said, "To you has been given to know the secrets of the kingdom of God; but for others they are in parables, so that seeing they may not see, and hearing they may not understand. Now the parable is this: The seed is the word of God. The ones along the path are those who have heard; then the devil comes along and takes away the word from their hearts, that they may not

believe and be saved. And the ones on the rock are those who, when they hear the word, receive it with joy; but these have no root, they believe for a while and in time of temptation fall away. And as for what fell among the thorns, they are those who hear, but as they go on their way they are choked by the cares and riches and pleasures of life, and their fruit does not mature. And as for that in the good soil, they are those who, hearing the word, hold it fast in an honest and good heart, and bring forth fruit with patience."

Matthew 13.1–9, 18–23
That same day Jesus went out of the house and sat beside the sea. And great crowds gathered about him, so that he got into a boat and sat there; and the whole crowd stood on the beach. And he told them many things in parables, saying: "A sower went out to sow. And as he sowed, some seeds fell along the path, and the birds came and devoured them. Other seeds fell on rocky ground, where they had not much soil, and immediately they sprang up, since they had no depth of soil, but when the sun rose they were scorched; and since they had no root they withered away. Other seeds fell upon thorns, and the thorns grew up and choked them. Other seeds fell on good soil and brought forth grain, some a hundredfold, some sixty, some thirty. He who has ears, let him hear. . . .

"Hear then the parable of the sower. When any one hears the word of the kingdom and does not understand it, the evil one comes and snatches away what was sown in his heart; this is what was sown along the path. As for what was sown on rocky ground, this is he who hears the word and immediately receives it with joy; yet he has no root in himself, but endures for a while, and then tribulation or persecution arises on account of the word, immediately he falls away. As for what was sown among thorns, this is he who hears the word, but the cares of the world and the delight in riches choke the word, and it proves unfruitful. As for what was sown on good soil, this is he who hears the word and understands it; he indeed bears fruit, and yields, in one case a hundredfold, in another sixty, and in another thirty."

The Parable of the Sower can be subject to a number of interpretations. According to Matthew, this is the first parable that Jesus ever spoke. Jesus is presented as walking near the seaside and a large crowd gathered around him so that he had to get into a boat and sit in it, while the whole crowd was beside the sea on land. Apparently to escape the great crowd pressing against him, Jesus went into a boat and there he taught and spoke. In the parable, Jesus presents the seed falling along the common ground and the birds are presented as devouring it. Second, the seed fell on rocky ground where there was little soil apparently, but basically this ground was not filled with stones but had some amount of earth over some rock. If the seed fell in this area, it would sprout, but when the sun rose, Jesus says the seed there would wither and die without moisture and nourishment to withstand the heat of the sun. Jesus, finally, says that the other seed fell among thorns, and the thorns grew up and choked it and it yielded no grain. Finally, Jesus says other seeds fell into good soil and brought forth grain, which greatly increased.

This story is presented in this fashion in the fourth chapter of Mark 4.1-9. In Luke 8.4-15, Jesus explains what he means here. He says to his disciples that he is giving them specific knowledge of the kingdom of God. He says that in this parable, the seed is the word of God. He says that the ones along the path are those who hear, but then the seed falls away and is taken by the devil from their hearts. The seed that falls on the rocky ground are those who hear the word and receive it with joy but since it cannot take root, the result is these persons believe for a time and then fall away. As for what falls on the thorns, these people hear but they proceed on their way, choked by the cares and riches of the world. Finally, Jesus says that when the seed falls in good soil, these people hear the word and hold it fast in an honest and good heart and bring forth good fruit with patience.

This parable needs some interpretation. The seed is the Word of God, and its purpose is to bring human persons to God and to relationship with God. What happens with the Word of God depends on the individual soul, mind, and person. When it falls on the wayside ground, these people simply hear the Word of God, but what was sown in their hearts never takes root. It is as if the Word of God never came to them. Where the seed falls on rocky ground, this may be said to stand for those who may give lip service to faith but it has no meaning and takes no root in them. They may think about so-called "religion" but go on to other things without much thought to Christ or his Word, one way or the other. In sum, they are lazy and unmotivated, and they forget. As for the seed, or Word, that fell among the thorns, this may be thought to stand for those who hear the Word and think about it for a while and then go on to other things. Their life crowds out the Word of God and Christ. The fourth group of people are the people who hear, understand, and absorb the Word of God.

This parable is extremely timely and relevant. The various different kinds of ground that are described here are the different types of people that we encounter in the world. Jesus says that the wayside ground is those people whom the Word of God never reaches despite their hearing it. The rocky ground is those people whom the Word of God temporarily reaches but they pay little attention or none. The thorny ground, as I said, is those souls whose other activities crowd out Christ and his word. Finally, there are those who are receptive, prescient, and open-minded and hear the Word of God and understand it and apply it to their lives.

We all know there are different types of people in the world who we may be very nice to, kind to, and even in a certain sense love others, and nothing happens, for whatever reason. They are like the different kinds of ground or soil in this parable. They have souls or things in their lives that do not permit a loving relationship or, better put, are self-centered, unthinking, and shallow. There are those who minds are shut to anybody but themselves. There are those who are so busy with themselves that they crowd out, or have no use for, Christ. Jesus says here that it is not our fault, or his fault, that we are not received by another or that he is not received. It is that person's soul makeup that literally walls them in 0and prevents them from receiving the love of others or, ultimately, the love of Christ. They cannot include anything beyond themselves, whether their life crowds out the life of Christ and others, which is the thorny ground, or they are so limited and shallow that they cannot receive the Word of God, which are those with the rocky ground, or those whose souls, are like the wayside ground, where the Word of God takes no root.

It is a sad state of affairs that Jesus Christ, who offers ultimate love, the ultimate relationship, eternal joy, and eternal and abundant life is constantly faced with souls to whom he presents himself and reaches out, but there are only a few who are sufficiently intelligent and open-minded and have the mental grasp to take up what is offered, which is nothing less than abundant and joyful eternal life and eternal love forever.

Chapter 2
The Parable of the Patient Husbandman

Mark 4.26–29
And he said, "The kingdom of God is as if a man should scatter seed upon the ground, and should sleep and rise night and day, and the seed should sprout and grow, he knows not how. The earth produces of itself, first the blade, then the ear. But when the grain is ripe, at once he puts in the sickle, because the harvest has come."

The Parable of the Patient Husbandman is somewhat difficult to grasp. Jesus says that the kingdom of God is akin to a man's scattering seed on the ground which seed then sprouts, but the husbandman does not know exactly why. Jesus seems to say here that God's actions in the world and the way they will happen are not predictable, but gradual.

The parable says that no one can make the Word of God grow; the process of God's kingdom's taking root and growing is unpredictable and will happen in God's own time. Just as we cannot predict when we or anyone else will grow into Christ or when Christ will return in Final Judgment, this parable says that the process of opening minds and hearts goes along gradually and slowly. The time will come, this parable says, as mandated by the cosmic Christ, the God who rules the heavens and earth, who is the God of history and all human events. As Christ is presented to the world and the Gospel is presented, we cannot know in whom it will take root or when, but this parable says in that fullness of time and God's own time, the Kingdom of God will come and make itself known in the world.

The seed that matures into the blade and then the ear represents the souls of human persons, and when those souls are fully transformed and grown into Christ, they will join him in the Resurrection and in the new heavens and new earth. The harvest in this parable, I think, stands for those people who, at the end of time, have heard the Word of God and have been transformed into sons of God in Christ and, at the end of time, are joining him and proceeding into eternal life in Christ and the Trinity.

Chapter 3
The Parable of the Mustard Seed

Mark 4.30–32
And he said, "With what can we compare the kingdom of God, or what parable shall we use for it? It is like a grain of mustard seed, which, when sown upon the ground, is the smallest of all the seeds on earth; yet when it is sown it grows up and becomes the greatest of all shrubs and puts forth large branches, so that the birds of the air can make nests in its shade."

Matthew 13.31–32
Another parable he put before them, saying, "The kingdom of heaven is like a grain of mustard seed which a man took and sowed in his field; it is the smallest of all seeds, but when it has grown it is the greatest of shrubs and becomes a tree, so that the birds of the air come and make nests in its branches."

Luke 13.18–19
He said therefore, "What is the kingdom of God like? And to what shall I compare it? It is like a grain of mustard seed which a man took and sowed in his garden; and it grew and became a tree, and the birds of the air made nests in its branches."

The Parable of the Mustard Seed is found in both the Gospel of Mark, the Gospel of Matthew, and the Gospel of Luke. I think the significance of Jesus' Parable of the Mustard Seed is that the smallest, for God, not only becomes the greatest but is the greatest. In Palestine, the mustard seed was associated with the smallest of all things. The parable revolves around the idea, or notion, that this very small seed grows into the largest of bushes.

We must remember that the disciples were really quite humble in background, fishermen or, if you will, working folk. This parable makes the point that the world, and its values, are staggeringly deceptive. The world eludes and bewilders us, fooling us into thinking that wealth, power, appearance, and glitz are big and important. Jesus makes the point here that every person has the potential to become an eternal being or, better put, has the potential for greatness. God is not fooled. He sees in the least of us, the greatest of persons and souls. Further, Jesus teaches here that the Church can be small and insignificant in one place and generation and, being a living organism, can grow into greatness in another place or time.

I think the point of the parable is that we are not to be fooled by the world and its appearances. Christ knows, and God knows, that every person and every soul has the potential to be an eternal being in the course of time, a being with the growth or potential to be something far beyond the grasp of the evaluation system of the world, which judges by wealth and power. That person who has the potential to be an eternal being in communion and relationship with Christ, Jesus says, has moved to a plane and level that is beyond and unattainable to with what the world has to offer.

Also, Jesus counters here the attitude that is true for many people in our present generation in the modem world, that the Church is irrelevant, is some sort of fairy tale and some sort of foolishness. Jesus says here that the Church will always be here, will always be in growth, and will eventually grow to overcome the values of the world. It will be a place where all people will come and be remade into something beyond what they possibly thought they could be. The smallest person, Jesus says, is the greatest. In a Church under the trees in Africa or in a store front in urban America, the Church becomes the greatest of shrubs and the greatest of trees.

Chapter 4
The Parable of the Wicked Husbandmen

Mark 12.1–11
And he began to speak to them in parables. "A man planted a vineyard, and set a hedge around it, and dug a pit for the wine press, and built a tower, and let it out to tenants, and went into another country. When the time came, he sent a servant to the tenants to get from them some of the fruit of the vineyard. And they took him and beat him and sent him away empty-handed. Again he sent to them another servant, and they wounded him in the head and treated him shamefully. And he sent another and him they killed; and so with many others, some they beat and some they killed. He had still one other, a beloved son; finally he sent him to them, saying, 'They will respect any son.' But those tenants said to one another, 'This is the heir; come, let us kill him, and the inheritance will be ours.' And they took him and killed him and cast him out of the vineyard. What will the owner of the vineyard do? He will come and destroy the tenants and give the vineyard to others. Have you not read this scripture: 'The very stone which the builders rejected has become the head of the corner; this was the Lord's doing, and it is marvelous in our eyes?'"

Matthew 21.33–44
"Hear another parable. There was a householder who planted a vineyard, and set a hedge around it, and dug a winepress in it, and built a tower, and let it out to tenants, and went into another country. When the season of fruit drew near, he sent his servants to the tenants, to get his fruit; and the tenants took his servants and beat one, killed another, and stoned another. Again he sent other servants, more than the first; and they did the same to them. Afterward he sent his son to them, saying, 'They will respect my son.' But when the tenants saw the son, they said to themselves, 'This is the heir; come, let us kill him and have his inheritance.' And they took him and cast him out of the vineyard and killed him. When therefore the owner of the vineyard comes, what will he do to those

tenants?" They said to him, "He will put those wretches to a miserable death, and let out the vineyard to other tenants who will give him the fruits in their seasons."

Luke 20. 9–18
And he began to tell the people this parable: "A man planted a vineyard, and let it out to tenants, and went into another country for a long while. When the time came, he sent a servant to the tenants, that they should give him some of the fruit of the vineyard; but the tenants beat him and sent him away empty-handed. And he sent another servant; him also they beat and treated shamefully and sent him away empty-handed. And he sent yet a third; this one they wounded and cast out. Then the owner of the vineyard said, 'What shall I do? I will send my beloved son; it may be they will respect him.' But when the tenants saw him, they said to themselves, 'This is the heir; let us kill him, that the inheritance may be ours.' And they cast him out of the vineyard and killed him. What then will the owner of the vineyard do to them? He will come and destroy those tenants, and give the vineyard to others." When they heard this, they said, "God forbid!" But he looked at them and said, "What then is this that is written: 'The very stone which the builders rejected has become the heard of the corner'? Everyone who falls on that stone will be broken into pieces; but when it falls on any one it will crush him."

I shall now give what I think is the point, or proper interpretation, of the Parable of the Wicked Husbandmen. This parable may be found in all three synoptic gospels: Mark 12, 1–11; Matthew 21, 33–34; Luke 20, 9–18. The story is basically the same in each of the gospels. Jesus states that a man plants a vineyard, digs a wine press in it, builds a tower, and then goes to another country for some time and lets it out to tenants. When the time comes to get some of the fruit from the vineyard, he sends his servant, or servants, to the tenants to get some of the fruit of the vineyard. Jesus states that the servants are beaten and attacked. Then, finally, the owner of the vineyard sends his beloved son, hoping they would respect his son, but when the tenants see the son, they take him and kill him. In Luke, Chapter 20, three servants are sent and beaten.

Jesus asks those listening to him what they think the owner would do to those tenants, and they say to him the owner would put those people to death and let out the vineyard to other tenants. Jesus concludes this parable with the statement that the stone the builders rejected has become the head of the corner. This parable is told close after Jesus" entry into Jerusalem related in Luke, Chapter 19, when Jesus enters on a donkey and cleanses the temple, driving out the money changers.

How are we to interpret this parable then? The vineyard represents humanity, and its master is God. Jesus says that the vineyard tenants are perhaps those who have control in our society. The servants are those people in the world who seek to serve, assist, and help. In this parable, the people who seek to serve and help are beaten and killed by the tenants of the vineyard.

I think Jesus says in this parable that God and Christ sets all of us in a vineyard and gives us the opportunity, as he did to the tenants, to live our lives in righteousness. He sends his servants, who might be the righteous men of the age, perhaps the priests and ministers of our time, to gather the fruit of humanity and the goodness it produces. As we all know, not only are the good men and righteous men beaten and attacked here in the world as they often are but the son of God, Christ himself, is killed by the tenants.

God originally gave humanity a Garden of Eden and was prepared to give them joy and love for eternity in relation to him. Adam and Eve rejected this chance by their disobedience. In the same way, we are the tenants in this parable of the vineyard, which is our life on earth. Jesus sends his servants to the world, and they are attacked and, ultimately, his only beloved son is crucified.

Jesus says here, and concludes, that those who reject him will have the result that eternal life will be given to others. The meaning of the parable is that in rejecting his claim, the son of God and Christ will become the head. The world destroys the good continually. God continually sends his servants to the world and the world seeks their destruction. We have seen this again and again. The world is controlled by continuous sin and evil. This sin is so great that the good are rejected and even the son of God was rejected and suffered a horrible death out of his love for humanity. In that rejection, he is raised to become the head, and the parable says, unequivocally, that those who are unmoved and wicked will be destroyed, and a new cosmic order will emerge, to be given to and inherited by the righteous.

Chapter 5
The Parable of the Budding Fig Tree

Mark 13.28–37
"From the fig tree learn its lesson: as soon as its branches becomes tender and puts forth its leaves, you know that summer is near. So also, when you see these things taking place, you know that he is near, at the very gates. Truly, I say to you, this generation will not pass away before all these things take place. Heaven and earth will pass away, but my words will not pass away. But of that day or that hour no one knows, not even the angels in heaven, nor the Son, but only the Father. Take heed, watch; for you do not know when the time will come. It is like a man going on a journey. When he leaves home, he puts his servants in charge, each with his work, and commands the doorkeeper to be on the watch. Watch therefore for you do not know when the master of the house will come, in the evening or at midnight, or at cockcrow, or in the morning—lest he come suddenly and find you asleep. And what I say to you I say to all: 'Watch.'"

Matthew 24.32–39
"From the fig tree learn its lesson: as soon as its branch becomes tender and puts forth its leaves, you know that summer is near. So also, when see all these things, you know that he is near, at the very gates. Truly, I say to you, this generation will not pass away till all these things take place. Heaven and earth will pass away, but my words will not pass away. But of that day and hour no one knows, not even the angels of heaven, nor the Son, but the Father only. As were the days of the Noah, so will be the coming of the Son of Man. For as in those days before the flood, they were eating and drinking, marrying and giving in marriage, until the day when Noah entered the ark, and they did not know until the flood came and swept them all away, so will be the coming of the Son of Man."

The Budding Fig Tree 14

Luke 21.29–33
And he told them a parable: "Look at the fig tree, and all the trees; as soon as they come out in leaf, you see for yourselves and know that the summer is near. So also, when you see these things taking place, you know that the kingdom of God is near. Truly, I say to you, this generation will not pass away till all has taken place. Heaven and earth will pass away, but my words will not pass away."

The Parable of the Budding Fig Tree, like the parable of the Wicked Husbandmen, again is found in all three synoptic gospels: Mark 13.28-37, Matthew 24.32-39, and Luke 21.29-33. In this parable, Jesus says that when the branches of the fig tree become tender and put forth leaves, summer is approaching. In the same way, he says he is near at the very gates. He says that this generation will not pass away before these things take place, and heaven and earth will pass away, but not his words. He says of the day or the hour, no one knows, but he tells us to watch, for we do not know when the time will come.

In Mark, he says that it is like a man going on a journey who leaves his home, puts his servants in charge, and commands the doorkeeper to be on watch. He says of himself that no one knows when the master of the house will come and finds you asleep. In Matthew, he recalls the days of Noah when people were engaged in their pleasures until Noah entered the ark, and that no one knew what would happen until the flood came and swept everyone away. He says the same will be true in the coming of the Son of Man.

This parable is a warning. What Jesus says here is that there will be a time when this world and our lives and everything will end. Jesus says here that we do not know when he will come and call us to account for what we have done in our lives, good or bad. He says that only God the Father knows when he will return and take charge and render judgment. We may think at that time that we are the important ones. We may think that not only are we acceptable but we are great because of our wealth, our intellect, or whatever else we wish to pin on ourselves, to make us something to others and to ourselves.

Jesus says this world will come to a conclusion, and we do not know when it will happen when he chooses to do so and comes back,. He says he can come and the world be remade and restored, but this can happen at any second. He tells us to watch, because the second when he chooses to return to this troubled world, we will be called to judgment. He says here we can hide nothing from him, and when he comes the x-ray and light of his judgment and his forgiveness will be directed to us and we will know who we truly were, and are, in our lives. He tells us to watch because we will never know the second this will occur.

What can we say of the lesson in this parable? We can only say this: that every second of our lives is critical in the use we make of it. Every second of our lives we can be the remade and restored human being in the world that we are capable of being. For this reason, Jesus tells us be careful, because at the second of his return, we will be revealed fully as persons. Nothing will save us, whether our wealth, our intellectual ability, or whatever we set about to take pride in, and whatever idols we set up to worship in place of the love of Christ and his undying mercy and forgiveness. He tells us to watch because there will be no escape at the very second. At that second, the drama of this world will come to an end, the play will come to a conclusion. He tells us we do not know when this will happen, but he warns us that we must be in a continual state of preparedness.

Chapter 6
The Parable of the Doorkeeper

Mark 13.33–37
"Take heed, watch; for you do not know when the time will come. It is like a man going on a journey, when he leaves home and puts his servants in charge, each with his work, and commands the doorkeeper to be on the watch. Watch therefore—for you do not know when the master of the house will come, in the evening or at midnight, or at cockcrow, or in the morning—lest he come suddenly and find you asleep. And what I say to you I say to all: 'Watch.'"

Luke 12.35–40
"Let your loins be girded and your lamps burning, and be like men who are waiting for their master to come home from the marriage feast, so that they may open to him at once when he comes and knocks. Blessed are those servants whom that master finds awake when he comes; truly, I say to you, he will gird himself and have them sit at table, and he will come and serve them. If he comes in the second watch, or in the third, and finds them so, blessed are those servants! But know this, that if the householder had known at what hour the thief was coming, he would not have left his house to be broken into. You also must be ready; for the Son of Man is coming at an unexpected hour."

The Parable of the Doorkeeper has great similarity to the previous parable in which I offered an analysis and interpretation (the Parable of the Budding Fig Tree). In the Parable of the Doorkeeper, found in Mark 13.33–37 and Luke 12.35–40, Jesus says to watch. In Mark, he says it is like a man going on a journey who leaves home and puts his servants in charge and commands the doorkeeper to be on watch. He says therefore to watch for you do not know when the master of the house will come, and when he comes, whether in the evening, at midnight, at cockcrow, or in the morning, at that point, when he comes, you should not be asleep.

In Luke 12.35–40, Jesus says to keep your loins girded and your lamps burning, and be like men who are waiting for their master to come home from the marriage feast so that they may open to him when he comes and knocks. Jesus says that those servants are blessed whom the master finds awake when he comes. He says he will gird himself and have them sit at the table and will come and serve them. He says that if the master comes in the second or third watch and finds the servants so, those servants are blessed. Jesus adds that if the householder had known at what hour the thief was coming, he would not have left his house to be broken into. Jesus concludes that you must be ready, for the Son of Man is coming at an unexpected hour.

As I said, the import of this parable is somewhat similar to the previous parable I offered an interpretation of, in the sense that the parable here, known as the Parable of the Doorkeeper, concerns itself with the return of Christ. The meaning of the parable, I think, can be readily understood and interpreted. Essentially, Jesus says that one does not know when God, in him, will return. In Mark, he says it is like a man going on a journey who puts people in charge. In Luke, he says that the master is returning from the marriage feast. He tells us that we, the servants, or the doorkeeper, must be ready for his return.

It is extremely significant that in Luke he says that, when he does return, and we the servants sit at the table, he will serve them and us. In Luke, he tells us to be ready for his unexpected return. He says that had the householder known when the thief was coming, he would not have left his house. He warns us, in Luke and Mark, that we must be ready at any moment to be called into account as persons. Or better put, he tells us, in this parable that we do not know when our lives will end and when our little drama in our lives will be put aside. He tells us to be ready at all times, again, because we will never know when he will come and restore human beings fully to the joy and love in personal relation to Christ and God that is possible for all of us, or whether another fate will await us, and we do not know what it will be, precisely. There could be grace and forgiveness on the one hand and, on the other, eternal death, isolation, and loneliness forever could be the portion that awaits us.

Again, in this parable, he says we do not know when he, the master of the world and the ultimate master of all humanity, will return. He says that if we are found to be ready when he returns, he will come and serve us. I always remember, and will always remember, that at the last supper the Son of God washed the feet of his disciples, offering us an understanding, not only of God in Christ, but of what we should be as human beings. He tells us that he is not about power, not about wealth, and not about importance, but about serving and service.

As in the other parable I previously spoke of and attempted to understand, he tells us, in the Parable of the Doorkeeper, that in every second of our lives, we must be prepared for a face to face relationship with him. What will be the outcome, we do not know, but he tells us we must be ready at all times, not only for his return, but for the end of our lives when he does return as we know our lives, at that point. We must be prepared for his return because we must know that, with his piercing vision, like an x-ray, we will be revealed as we actually are, not with our fake self-importance, but with an understanding through him and in him, of what we have become, who we are, and what decisions we have made in the course of our lives. Every second of our lives we are confronted with the opportunity for moral and spiritual development. When the end comes, we will know who we are, what we have made of ourselves, and we will understand in him and through him, our actual being, as it actually is.

Chapter 7
The Parable of Going Before the Judge

Matthew 5.25–26
"Make friends quickly with your accuser while you are going with him to court, lest your accuser hand you over to the judge, and the judge to the guard, and you be put in prison; truly, I say to you, you will never get out till you have paid the last penny."

Luke 12.57–59
"And why do you not judge for yourselves what is right? As you go on with your accuser before the magistrate, make an effort to settle with him on the way, lest he drag you to the judge, and the judge hand you over to the officer, and the officer put you in prison. I tell you, you will never get out till you have paid the very last copper."

This parable concerns going before the Church. It is found in Matthew 25.25–26 and Luke 12.57–59. In this parable, Jesus tells us that our lives will be judged. If we live righteously, we will be judged with righteousness and humanity.

He tells us that if our lives have reached a crisis point, we should reach an agreement and be reconciled. If in our lives, we have had differences, disputes, and moral issues, he tells us to be reconciled with our enemies and even with those who have opposed us and possibly hurt us. The alternative is a judgment on us, he tells us. If we trust in our own feelings and efforts about our lives, and do not reach an understanding and agreement with people who may oppose us and hurt us and not reconcile with them, we may suffer at the hands of justice. He warns us not to wait till the last moment where there are issues concerning our possible condemnation and wrongdoing. He suggests reconciliation, and perhaps forgiveness, with our enemies and accusers. He tells us that unless we do this, we face a total judgment on our actions that could perhaps be disastrous. He says we cannot trust in our own thoughts about ourselves and our own assuredness about the rightness of our position. He says here that, as we live, we must be reconciled with all and forgive all for the injuries they have done us. If we are not so reconciled and depend on our own concept of our own righteousness and the supposed rightness of our position, our fate can be far worse than we can possibly anticipate. No one can face judgment. No one of us can stand before the judge.

He tells that as we live our lives we must yield in love to all, not holding grudges, but seeking love and friendship, even with our enemies. Certainly, he says in Luke, that when we reach the last moment of our lives, we will be judged. He says in Luke that we are shortly in our lives to possibly appear before the judge, unless we reach a state of love and forgiveness with all. The alternative, Luke suggests, is a test and condemnation before the judge and imprisonment. Both Matthew and Luke, in this parable, warn us that, as we live our lives, we must live our lives with accommodation of all, understanding of all, and forgiveness of all who may injure us, including our accusers. If we do not so live our lives, we will be subject to the same treatment we have afforded others, as we have lived the course of our lives. If we have lived with others without reconciliation, love and forgiveness, we will be handed over to the judge, and there may be no hope.

Chapter 8
The Parable of the Two Houses

Matthew 7.24–27
"Everyone then who hears these word of mine and does them will be like a wise man who built his house upon the rock; and the rain fell, and the floods came, and the winds blew and beat upon that house, but it did not fall, because it had been founded on the rock. And every one who hears these words of mine and does not do them will be like a foolish man who built his house upon the sand; and the rain fell, and the floods came, and the winds blew and beat against that house, and it fell; and great was the fall of it."

Luke 6.47–49
"Everyone who comes to me and hears my words and does them, I will show you what he is like: he is like a man building a house, who dug deep, and laid the foundation upon rock; and when a flood arose, the stream broke against the house, and could not shake it because it had been well built. But he who hears and does not do them is like a man who built a house on the ground without a foundation, against which the stream broke, and immediately it fell, and the ruin of that house was great."

In the Parable of the Two Houses, found in Matthew 7.24–27 and Luke 6.47–49, Jesus tells us that those who hear and understand his message will be like a man who has built his house upon a rock or, as Luke says, dug deep and laid the foundation on the rock. Jesus says that when the rain fell, when the floods came, and the winds and rain broke against the house, they could not shake it. He says that everyone who hears his words and does not do them is like a foolish man who built his house upon the ground or the sand, without a foundation, and the rain fell, and the floods came, and the stream broke, and the house had a great fall.

In this parable, the message of Jesus, I think, is quite clear. Unless we heed and believe what he tells us, we are like the house built upon the sand that can be shaken. Should we in some way in our lives, either actually or implicitly build our lives on a false foundation, we will be swept away at the last and final judgment. In that sense, should we not live our lives in relation to him and his teaching with what we should do with our lives, the final judgment will sweep us away.

He tells us in this parable that he is the rock and foundation for authentic life. Should we built our lives on ourselves, our egos, our wealth, our looks, or whatever idol we may choose to erect, that will not work for us. When the end comes, we will be literally swept away and destroyed as persons.

As persons, we can only be in relation to him and his commands. Without him and without the rock and foundation he describes in this parable, we will have nowhere to go and will be literally taken away, if not taken away, but swept aside having failed to be fully human and not taking advantage of the opportunity and chance he offered us and offers to all, namely, to be and grow with him in sonship. The alternative, he tells us, should we not lay our lives in a foundation with him, in relationship to him, is abysmal failure and a fate of nothingness.

Chapter 9
The Parable of the Children in the Market

Matthew 11.16–19
"But to what shall I compare this generation? It is like children sitting in the market places and calling to their playmates, 'We piped to you, and you did not dance; we wailed, and you did not mourn.' For John came neither eating nor drinking, and they say, 'He has a demon'; the Son of Man came eating and drinking, and they say, 'Behold, a glutton and a drunkard, a friend of tax collectors and sinners!' Yet wisdom is justified by her deeds."

Luke 7.31–35
"To what then shall I compare the men of this generation, and what are they like? They are like children sitting in the market place and calling to one another, 'We piped to you, and you did not dance; we wailed, and you did not weep.' For John the Baptist has come eating no bread and drinking no wine and you say, 'He has a demon.' The Son of Man has come eating and drinking and you say, 'Behold, a glutton and a drunkard, a friend of tax collectors and sinners!' Yet wisdom is justified by all her children."

The Parable of the Children in the Market is found in Matthew 11.16–19 and Luke 7.31–35. In this parable in Matthew, Jesus says that this generation are like children sitting in the market and calling to their playmates and saying we piped to you and you did not dance and we wailed and you did not mourn. Jesus says that the present generation criticizes John, who came neither eating nor drinking, and says he has a demon. He says that the son of man came eating and drinking, and these same children say, behold a glutton and a drunkard, and a friend a tax collectors and sinners.

This parable is somewhat confusing, but I think I can offer a possible explanation. Human beings are refractory and contrary. Jesus says that we are like children who want this and want that. They say you did not dance with us when we played a tune, and you did not join us when we were sad. He says human nature criticizes goodness and perfection. John the Baptist, a prophet, is told he has a demon, and the very Son of God is criticized for being a glutton and a drunkard and a friend of tax collectors and sinners.

Jesus seems to say here that whatever goodness does is not enough and is rejected. If you do not do what we want, then we do not want it. If you are a great prophet, then you have a demon, and if the Son of God comes and offers love and forgiveness to sinners and the outcasts of society, he is criticized and condemned. It seems that human beings cannot have what they want, and what they want is mysterious. Jesus tells us that people are like children, asking for this, and asking for that, and condemning this and that which should be accepted and loved. Jesus says here that human nature is often twisted, crooked, and wrong in its judgments and choices. Jesus tells us here that people are always making the wrong turn and making the wrong choice, merely thinking of their own choices and expectations.

In this parable, Jesus exhibits great psychological insight into failed human nature. We all know, and he tells us, that we are like children, solely concerned with what we want of others and not offering anything to others, other than our desire to do what we want. He offers great psychological insight into how people reject, consistently and inexplicably, what is good for them. In fact, Jesus says that human nature adulates and respects power and importance and has little use for humility and goodness. Jesus very, very pointedly tells us that people find something in the good to not take and, ultimately, we know that saints have been tortured, martyred.

It is the ultimate resolution in this parable that the only begotten Son of God was rejected by human beings, tortured, and killed when all he did was good, healing, helping, loving and befriending. People see demons in prophets and criticize what should not be criticized but should be respected, namely, that the son of God chose love and friendship with the outcasts of society. Jesus, in this parable, tells us that what is good is often subject to attack, rejection, and criticism. Children want what they want, and if they do not get what they want, they are disappointed. Jesus tells us in this parable that human nature is like that nature of children: contrary, refractory, and often making the wrong choices. It is somewhat ironic that human nature certainly made the wrong choice with respect to Jesus, and has done so with many others.

Chapter 10
The Parable of the Return of the Unclean Spirit

Matthew 12.43–45
"When the unclean spirit has gone out of a man, he passes through waterless places seeking rest, but he finds none. Then he says, 'I will return to my house from which I came.' And when he comes he finds it empty, swept, and put in order. Then he goes and brings with him seven other spirits more evil than himself and they enter and dwell there; and the last state of that man becomes worse than the first. So shall it be also with this evil generation."

Luke 11.24–26
"When the unclean spirit has gone out of a man, he passes through waterless places seeking rest and finding none he says, 'I will return to my house from which I came.' And when he comes he finds it swept and put it in order. Then he goes and brings seven other spirits more evil than himself, and they enter and dwell there and the last state of that man becomes worse than the first."

The Parable of the Return of the Unclean Spirit is found in Matthew 12.43–45 and Luke 11.24–26. In this parable in Matthew, Jesus says that when an unclean spirit, or perhaps better understood demon, passes through waterless places, seeking rest, but finding none he says, "I will return to my house from which I came." And when he finds it empty, he goes and brings with him several other demons, and they enter and dwell there. He says that this last stated man is worse than the first. In Matthew, there is a last sentence that says it shall be thus with this evil generation, and that the last state of that man will be worse than the first.

This parable is somewhat difficult to interpret, but I would like to offer my view of it. Jesus says here that within us, when the evil has been expelled, understood as a demon and understood as wickedness, unless that person becomes in relationship to Christ, the demon can return, and with seven other demons more evil than himself. When our evil nature has been decimated and the evil expelled, it must be replaced with the love of Christ, and that love must have taken over our being. If the evil and wickedness may reside in all of us, it will be taken over sevenfold with greater wickedness and evil and we will be far worse off as persons than we were. We cannot be empty shells and tombs. Unless we live in Christ and with Christ, the evil and demon that had formerly resided within us will again take us over and will increase many times over in our souls and in even in our bodies. There is no alternative to Christ this parable tells us. Without him we face only sevenfold wickedness taking us over.

Chapter 11
The Parable of the Tares Among the Wheat

Matthew 13.24–30
Another parable he put before them, saying, "The kingdom of heaven may be compared to a man who sowed good seed in his field; but while men were sleeping, his enemy came and sowed weeds among the wheat and went away. So when the plants came up and bore grain, then the weeds appeared also. And the servants of the householder came and said to him, 'Sir, did you not sow good seed in your field? How then has it weeds?' He said to them, 'An enemy has done this.' The servants said to him, 'Then do you want us to go and gather them?' But he said, 'No, lest in gathering the weeds you root up the wheat along with them. Let both grow together until the harvest; and at harvest time I will tell the reapers, Gather the weeds first and bind them in bundles to be burned, but gather the wheat into my barn.'"

The Parable of the Tares Among the Wheat is found in Matthew 13.24–30. In this parable, Jesus says that the Kingdom of Heaven can be compared to a man who sowed good seed in his field but, while men were sleeping, his enemy came and sowed weeds among the wheat and went away. Jesus says in this parable that when the plants came up and bore grain the weeds appeared also. The servants of the household then came and said, "Sir, did you not grow good seed in your field? How then has it weeds?" He then said to them that an enemy did this. The servants are then related to say to the master, "Do you want us to go gather them?" but the master says not to do this, since they would root up the wheat along with the weeds. The master then concludes with a statement that both should grow together and, at the harvest, he will tell the reapers to gather the weeds first and bind them in bundles to be burned, but gather the wheat into his barn.

This parable is somewhat difficult to understand. Jesus seems to say here that the world consists of good seed, or good people, mixed with bad. Jesus says that we are not to make a judgment here immediately, since there is both good and bad in the world. Jesus seems to say here that also, in our lives, we may sow good, but Satan may also seek to infect and corrupt those who do good and sow good. Jesus says here that we are not to make an immediate judgment call on persons, lest we make an incorrect judgment. Rather, he says that we are to wait and be patient until there is some sort of final situation where the weeds will be separated from the tares, bound in bundles to be burned, and the righteous people gathered together.

Jesus tells us that the world is a place of confusion, where in the face of goodness and love, evil and corruption exist and grow hand in hand. The world was created good but human nature at the beginning was corrupted and fell. There cannot be a separation immediately of who is good and who is bad, and who will be with Christ and who will not. Jesus says here that we have to be patient. At some point, there will be a gathering and separation but we must wait.

There is good in the world together with bad and evil. Jesus says here we cannot make the separation by ourselves or make a judgment on others, but he does tell us that there will be a separation and gathering. The corrupt and evil will be destroyed, and the good and evil will be gathered together and preserved. He does tell us that we must be patient and await the final outcome and not make a quick judgment but await the final judgment by the ultimate judge.

Chapter 12
The Parable of the Leaven

Matthew 13.33
He told them another parable. "The kingdom of heaven is like leaven which a woman took and hid in three measures of flour, till it was all leavened."

Luke 13.20–21
And again he said, "To what shall I compare the kingdom of God? It is like leaven which a woman took and hid in three measures of flour, till it was all leavened."

This parable, the so-called Parable of the Leaven, is found in two of the synoptic gospels: Matthew 13.33 and Luke 13.20–21. In each of these instances, Jesus says that the kingdom of God is like leaven which a woman took and hid in three measures of flour until it was leavened. Matthew 13.44 (which is discussed in more detail in the next chapter) is a slightly different version, but states that the kingdom of heaven is like treasure hidden in a field, which a man finds and covers up and then, in his joy, sells all that he has and buys that field.

The idea behind these metaphors of leaven is that the treasure spoken of in Matthew 13.44 is, so to say, the working of the Christian influence and Christ's influence in society and, like the leaven in the dough, is a slow and imperceptible situation. Jesus says here that at first there is nothing, but then in the course of time, there is growth and development, that is to say spiritual growth and development. One can also speculate that this parable not only addresses spiritual growth but possibly an improved society, and the outcome, in this slow process, is a slow and imperceptible moral, and possibly more just, society.

The idea, I think, in this short statement of Christ's is that the kingdom of God, like the leaven, will slowly grow in the world , have an influence, and charge and slowly grow until the fullness of time when there is a new world order. It will take time, Jesus says in this parable; it will be a slow process, like the leaven and flour that the woman took and hid. Both the outside world and the inner person will slowly grow and improve. In a sense, the leaven is a kind of slow revolution in bringing about improvement and change, both in the person, and in the world surrounding him. Perhaps Jesus may be thought to have said in this parable that as the leaven grows in the flour, injustices and inequities will slowly be eradicated, and there will both be a revolution of all men and women and perhaps, as a result, a sort of new world and new world order in which economic injustices and inequities will be eliminated and we will all be better persons with it.

Chapter 13
The Parable of the Treasure

Matthew 13.44
"The kingdom of heaven is like treasure hidden in a field, which a man found and covered up; then in his joy he goes and sells all that he has and buys that field."

In Matthew 13.44 Jesus analogizes the kingdom of heaven to a treasure hidden in a field, which a man finds and covers up; then in his joy he goes and sells all that he has and buys this field. This particular parable can be succinctly interpreted or understood. The first sentence of the parable sets up a comparison to a man's unexpected find of a treasure. Perhaps, in some way, people find Christ and Jesus in an accidental fashion. They may hear someone presenting the Christian message or in some way Jesus enters that man's life like the treasure, accidently. But then, having discovered the value of who Christ is and can be to him, the man sells all he has.

The man is said to sell everything he has to have that treasure in the field, which he unexpectedly and accidentally found. It is significant that when the treasure is found, the man realizes its great significance and importance to him and not only hides it and covers it up so that he may have it all for himself but he sells everything that he has to have that treasure. The parable is the recognition by the man of Christ and the kingdom of heaven. The man's recognition is so piercing and compelling that he gives everything he has to have that treasure and possess for himself that field.

In a sense the parable is somewhat puzzling since the man's actions here are extremely selfish and reflect an intense self-involvement. Having found the treasure, the man is not inclined to share it or even show it to anyone. Clearly, the treasure, Jesus says, is hidden in the field for him and is the kingdom of heaven. One may speculate that this parable reflects a man who is extremely intelligent about what he has found, but on the other hand he is unwilling that anyone else find it. In fact, his desire for the treasure is so great that he is willing to sell everything he has to purchase the field. In a sense, the man is very smart in seeing the value of Christ in his life. On the other hand, apparently, he only thinks of himself and having the treasure for himself. In that sense, Jesus tells us that we should recognize who he is and what he says to us, but on the other hand, I find it somewhat puzzling and do not understand the man's taking everything for himself and apparently being unwilling to share the gospel with others.

Chapter 14
The Parable of the Pearl

Matthew 13.45
"Again, the kingdom of heaven is like a merchant in search of fine pearls, who, on finding one pearl of great value, went and sold all that he had and bought it."

The next parable is known as the Parable of the Pearl. This parable, found in Matthew 13.45, is similar in language and meaning to the parable of the treasure, which I have just related and analyzed. In the Parable of the Pearl, found only in Matthew, Jesus is represented as saying that the kingdom of heaven is like a merchant in search of fine pearls who, on finding one pearl of great value, sells all he has and buys it.

In this parable the man may be said to be the person who is searching and looking. Perhaps the analogy here is that the merchant is not looking for something of material value, but something that could change his life and thinking or remake him as a person. The analogy, again, is that having found Christ, the person gives up everything and gives up all his material goods and buys it.

The idea of sacrifice is present here. Jesus says here that, like the merchant, we can search our entire lives for some truth or something to pin our lives on as human beings. Like us, when the merchant finally finds the pearl of great value, which is Christ, he is represented as giving up all his material goods to have Jesus. All of us, in our lives, are on a journey or a timeline. Each of us has a timeline and, in that timeline, Jesus tells us here we search for some truth or something that we can believe in. Jesus says here when we find him, like the merchant we may have to sacrifice things that we possess or even marital ties.

The interpretation is that when we finally find the answer in Christ, like the merchant, we may have to sacrifice everything to possess that pearl, which is Christ. He says to follow Christ is not easy and may involve sacrifice and persecution, but he says that for the person who knows who he is, he will, having been so discerning, give up everything for Christ.

Chapter 15
The Parable of the Seine-net

Matthew 13.47–50
"Again, the kingdom of heaven is like a net which was thrown into the sea and gathered fish of every kind; when it was full, men drew it ashore and sat down and sorted the good into vessels but threw away the bad. So it will be at the end of the age. The angels will come out and separate the evil from the righteous, and throw them into the furnace of fire; there men will weep and gnash their teeth."

In the Parable of the Seine, found in Matthew 13.47–50, Jesus relates that the kingdom of heaven is like a net which was thrown into the sea and gathered fish of every kind. Jesus says that when the net was full, men drew it ashore and sat down and sorted the good into vessels, but threw away the bad. Jesus concludes this parable with a statement that this is done so that the evil are separated from the righteous, and the evildoers are thrown into the furnace of fire where men will weep and gnash their teeth.

This parable is thought to be addressed to the disciples. In this parable, the kingdom of God, or his outreach to the world, is to all men and women of every race, religion, and background. He gathers about, or reaches out, to everyone, but Jesus then says that, despite his wish and desire that all men be saved and have eternal life and joy with him, there will come a time for separation. Prior to this separation, he says the good are mixed with the bad. Jesus says that in God's time in judgment, the evil will be separated from the good and righteous and that evil men, religious hypocrites, will be separated from the people who have made good use of their lives.

Jesus and God cast a wide net and deeply wish that all men be saved. He is willing to give them a last moment of grace and repentance before they die, or

all of us die. Ultimately, he says that there will be a final judgment, and it will be God's judgment and not ours. The evil will be condemned to a furnace of fire where they will weep and gnash their teeth. They will weep and gnash their teeth not so much as for the physical suffering they will endure in the furnace of fire,
since I think the furnace of fire is only an analogy, but they will weep and gnash their teeth in their loneliness and separation from love, and the joy of eternal communion and eternal life with God and Christ. They will be condemned to weep and gnash their teeth, looking at the reward of the good and knowing their fate to be alone without love. They will surely know that there is no place safer from love than hell and condemnation, since love is only found in the presence of God and his only begotten son, Jesus Christ.

Chapter 16
The Parable of the Lost Sheep

Matthew 18.12–14
"What do you think? If a man has a hundred sheep and one of them has gone astray, does he not leave the ninety-nine on the mountains and go in search of the one that went astray? And if he finds it, truly I say to you, he rejoices over it more than over the ninety-nine that never went astray. So it is not the will of my Father who is in heaven that one of these little ones should perish."

Luke 15.3–7
So he told them this parable: "What man of you, having a hundred sheep, if he has lost one of them, does not leave ninety-nine in the wilderness and go after the one which is lost until he finds it? And when he has found it, he lays it on his shoulders, rejoicing. And when he comes home, he calls together his friends and his neighbors, saying to them, 'Rejoice with me, for I have found my sheep which was lost.' Just so, I tell you there will be more joy in heaven over one sinner who repents than over ninety-nine righteous persons who need no repentance."

This chapter reflects on the Parable of the Lost Sheep, found in Matthew 18. 12–14 and Luke 15. 3–7. In this parable, Jesus says that if a man has a hundred sheep and one of them is gone astray, he will leave ninety-nine on the mountain and go in search of the one that went astray. In Matthew Jesus says that when he has found the lost sheep, he rejoices more than over the ninety-nine that never went astray. Jesus says that it is not the will of the Father in Heaven that any of these little ones should perish. In Luke, Jesus adds that when he finds the lost sheep, he lays it on his shoulder, rejoicing, and when he comes home, he calls together his friends and neighbors saying to them, "Rejoice with me for I have found my sheep which was lost." Jesus concludes here, in Luke, that there will be more joy in heaven over one sinner who repents than over ninety-nine righteous persons who need no repentance. According to Luke, where the Parable of the Lost Sheep is found, the Pharisees had raised the issue of Jesus' receiving sinners into his house and into a personal, social relationship. In Matthew, the audience is the disciples.

My view of what Jesus is driving at in this parable is that there are a number of ways of interpreting this. Number one, Jesus instructs us that if there is someone whom we see as undesirable or in error, that person should be sought for and included in the community if he can be found and reached. The sheep who is lost is, quite clearly, the person in sin, or the sinner. Jesus says here that in the eyes of God every person has infinite value. That value is so infinite and significant that the most undesirable, unattractive, and corrupt person has equal value to the ninety-nine righteous persons, because that sinner is part of God's creation and is his child, so to speak. The value of anyone is so great that, however lost in sin, God seeks them out to be with him in the joy of heaven. That person may have been lost but, should that person be found and repent, the joy in heaven will be triple fold and manifold because someone who was lost, was found, and that person, who was formerly lost in sin, has as equal and compelling value to God as the so-called righteous.

Perhaps another interpretation can be put on this parable. The world rejects people who are unattractive, undesirable, or without power, wealth or status. Jesus seems to tell us here that, for God and Christ, their value may be greater than the others the world seems to value and put a value on. The evaluation that God and Christ places on the individual is the same wherever they may be, whether in the poverty of an African hut or a mansion on the gold coast of Long Island. Not only does he see no distinction but, perhaps, on the person who is lost and devalued in the world, he may see and place greater value.

Jesus says in Matthew that he wishes no one to die and wants everyone in every generation that has ever lived or will live to be with him in eternal communion and love. He says in Luke that there will be more happiness over one person who repents and can be with him than over the ninety-nine righteous persons who need no repentance.

The message in this parable is twofold. Number one, God places a tremendous value on each and every person who has ever lived or will live. Second, that value he places one each and every one of us is so great that when one person is rescued there will be greater joy in heaven than over the ninety-nine righteous persons who needed no repentance. He analogizes our relationship with him to the shepherd who cares for his sheep. That care for the shepherd is greater for the lost than those who are found.

Perhaps we can only understand the love of God and Christ in this parable by understanding the incalculable and massive love that God has for all people, regardless of race, wealth, sex, or appearance. His love is so great for the one lost that he tells us of the overwhelming value, love, and joy that exist in heaven for that one person who returns to heaven and is no longer lost.

Chapter 17
The Parable of the Unmerciful Servant

Matthew 18.23–35
"Therefore, the kingdom of heaven may be compared to a king who wished to settle accounts with his servants. When he began the reckoning, one was brought to him who owed him ten thousand talents; and as he could not pay, his lord ordered him to be sold, with his wife and children and all that he had, and payment to be made. So the servant fell on his knees, imploring him, 'Lord, have patience with me, and I will pay you everything.' And out of pity for him the lord of that servant released him and forgave him the debt. But that same servant, as he went out, came upon one of his fellow servants who owed him a hundred denarii; and seizing him by the throat he said, 'Pay what you owe.' So his fellow servant fell down and besought him, 'Have patience with me, and I will pay you.' He refused and went and put him in prison till he should pay the debt. When his fellow servants saw what had taken place, they were greatly distressed, and they went and reported to their lord all that had taken place. Then his lord summoned him and said to him, 'You wicked servant! I forgave you all that debt because you besought me; and should not you have had mercy on your fellow servant, as I had mercy on you?' And in anger his lord delivered him to the jailers, till he should pay all his debt. So also my heavenly Father will do to every one of you, if you do not forgive your brother from your heart."

The Parable of the Unmerciful Servant is found in the Gospel of Matthew 18.23–35. In that parable, Jesus says that the kingdom of heaven can be compared to a king who wished to settle accounts with his servants. When he began this process, one servant was brought to him who owed him ten thousand talents, and since he could not pay, his lord order him to be sold with his wife and children and all that he had and payment to be made. The servant is said to have fallen on his knees, "Lord, have patience with me and I will pay you everything." Out of pity for him the lord of that servant released him and forgave him the debt.

That same servant, as he went out, came upon one of his fellow servants, who owed him one hundred denarii, and seized him by the throat. "Pay what you owe." The servant is said to have fallen down and asked the lord to have patience with him and that he would pay him. The lord refused and put him in prison that he should pay the debt.

When his fellow servants saw what had taken place, they were very upset and reported to the lord all that had taken place. His lord then summoned the servant and said to him, "You are a wicked servant! I forgave you all the debt because you besought me and why is it you do not have mercy on your fellow servant as I had mercy on you." In anger, the lord delivered the servant to the jailors that he should pay all his debt. Jesus concluded with the statement, "So also my heavenly father will do to every one of you if you do not forgive your brother from your heart."

This parable stems from a question asked by Peter directed to Jesus that if his brother sins against him and if he forgives him seven times is that enough. I think the point of this parable is that we cannot receive or expect God's forgiveness and love unless we show forgiveness to our fellow men in our lives. Here, the king forgives the servant and releases his debt. Yet the servant did not do the same. Not even thinking that forgiveness was shown to him, he literally attacks his fellow servant and grasps him by the throat. The unforgiving servant here demanded conduct from others that he himself did not possess.

Jesus says that his lord forgave his debt but the response of the servant when confronted with the same was to place the debtor in prison and show no mercy. The servant here did not rise in his own life to what he pleaded for from his own lord, or better put, he had the same fault and was forgiven but not seeing that fault within himself either he did not know of or was not prepared to forgive another.

The lesson of this parable is that at the end of our lives we must first of all recognize our faults and need for forgiveness. We must realize and understand that we cannot expect God to forgive us unless in our lives, as we have lived our lives, we have shown forgiveness and mercy to our fellow human beings. Jesus tells us the measure of us as persons will be how in the course of our lives we have treated other people. Have we shown them love, given the opportunity? Have we shown them forgiveness? Have we shown them mercy? Jesus tells us that we must recognize that we need forgiveness from God for our failings, faults, and deficiencies, and we will not have that forgiveness, love, and mercy that we desperately need from God unless in the course of our lives we have done the same and conducted ourselves in the same fashion.

Chapter 18
The Parable of the Good Employer

Matthew 20.1–16
"For the kingdom of heaven is like a householder who went out early in the morning to hire laborers for his vineyard. After agreeing with the laborers for a denarius a day, he sent them into his vineyard. And going out about the third hour he saw others standing idle in the market place; and to them he said, 'You go into the vineyard too, and whatever is right I will give you.' So they went. Going out again about the sixth hour and the ninth hour, he did the same. And about the eleventh hour he went out and found others standing; and he said to them, 'Why do you stand here idle all day?' They said to him, 'Because no one has hired us.' He said to them, 'You go into the vineyard too.' And when the evening came, the owner of the vineyard said to his steward, 'Call the laborers and pay them their wages, beginning with the last, up to the first.' And when those hired about eleventh hour came, each of them received a denarius. Now when the first came, they thought they would receive more; but each of them also received a denarius. And on receiving it they grumbled at the householder, saying, 'These last worked only one hour, and you have made them equal to us who have borne the burden of the day and the scorching heat.' But he replied to one of them, 'Friend, I am doing you no wrong; did you not agree with me for a denarius? Take what belongs to you, and go; I choose to give to this last as I give to you. Am I not allowed to do what I choose with what belongs to me? Or do you begrudge my generosity?' So the last will be first, and the first last."

Chapter 18 of this book is called the Parable of the Good Employer, and it is found in Mathew 20.1–16. In this parable, Jesus says that the kingdom of heaven is like a householder who goes out early in the morning to hire laborers for his vineyard. After agreeing with the laborers on a denarius a day, he sends them into his vineyard. Going out about the third hour, he sees others standing idle in the marketplace. "You go into the vineyard too and whatever is right I will give you." The employer continues to do this hiring and at the eleventh hour, he finds others standing and asks them, "Why do you stand here idle all day?" and they say to him, "No one has hired us." He says to them, "You go into the vineyard too."

Jesus says that when the evening comes, the owner of the vineyard says to his steward, "Call the laborers and pay them their wages, beginning with the last, and up to the first." And when those hired about the eleventh hour come, each receives a denarius. And when the first come they think they will receive more but also receive a denarius." On receiving the same payment, they grumble at the householder, saying, "These last worked only one hour and you have made them equal to us who have borne the burden of the day and the scorching heat." The householder replies, "Friend, I am doing you no wrong. Did you not agree with me for a denarius?" The householder is related to say, "Take what belongs to you. I choose to give to this last as I gave to you." The householder says, "I'm allowed to do with what belongs to me, and ask do you begrudge my generosity," Jesus concludes with the statement, "The last shall be first and the first last."

This parable is lengthy and somewhat involved. The parable has to do with generosity. The people hired at the early hour complain to the householder that they had to work twelve hours in the heat while the others worked one hour in the cool of the evening and received the same pay. The earlier hired employees felt that, for the difficulty of their work, the length of time involved, and the difficult conditions in the heat, they should have been paid more. Here Christ, and God, show compassion and goodness. Jesus gives, like the employer, to all, even sinners, a share in eternal life with him in heaven.

Jesus says here that he will choose to include the last in the world, as well as the first. He says here that his generosity, love, and compassion cannot be predicted or measured out only to those who believe they are deserving of it for their righteousness, and not to the others, who seem to be undeserving of God's compassion, love, and goodness.

It is significant that the householder continues to hire laborers all day, in the same way that God offers his love and compassion in the end of time to everyone. God's love and compassion and forgiveness are not based on what we have done for one hour, but on his grace, love, and mercy.

Jesus ends with a sentence that it is not the standard of the world that governs his actions, but in fact the undesirable that he was accused of consorting with—publicans, sinners, and tax collectors—will be first, and those who think solely of their entitlement and self-importance in the world system will be last. Jesus says here to all of us that his grace, love, compassion, and forgiveness are infinitely available and are not offered to those who may have worked for it, but are given to the least and apparently undeserving.

In fact, in these actions of Christ and God, Jesus says that the undesirable and outcasts, whom he was criticized for socializing with, will be seen as first, and the power mongers and self-important will be last. Jesus seems to say here that his measure of human persons and his grace cannot be predicted or understood. He says and concludes that his mercy and love are so great, that not only will he offer it to the apparently least deserving, but there will be a judgment that those undeserving will be first.

Chapter 19

The Parable of the Two Sons

Matthew 21.28–32
"What do you think? A man had two sons; and he went to the first and said, 'Son, go and work in the vineyard today.' And he answered, 'I will not'; but afterward he repented and went. And he went to the second and said the same; and he answered, 'I go, sir,' but did not go. Which of the two did the will of his father?" They said, "The first." Jesus said to them, "Truly, I say to you, the tax collectors and the harlots go into the kingdom of God before you in the way of righteousness, and you did not believe him, but the tax collectors and the harlots believed him; and even when you saw it, you did not afterward repent and believe him."

In this Chapter 19 is presented the Parable of the Two Sons. This parable is related solely in the Gospel of Matthew 21.28–32. In this parable, Jesus says that a man has two sons and goes up to the first and says, "Son, go and work on the vineyard today." The son answers, "I will not," but afterward he repents and goes. The father then goes to his second son who says he will go but does not go. Jesus asks, "Which of the two did the will of his father." The reply was the first. Jesus concludes, "Truly I say to you, the tax collectors and harlots go into the kingdom of God before you in the way of righteousness when you did not believe him but the tax collectors did believe him, and even when you saw it, you did not afterward repent and believe him."

This parable, initially, reflects the acts of repentance of the first son who then went and worked in the vineyard and the false statement of the second son who said he would go and work in the vineyard but did not go. The question that Jesus raises here is who of the two did the will of his father.

I think the meaning of this parable is clear in its conclusion. The first son has an association with the outcasts and sinners that Jesus was accused of associating with. As for the second son, it is not clear who he stands for except that he is a son who lies to his father and is therefore akin to the scribes and Pharisees whom Jesus saw as the religious hypocrites of the day.

Jesus says that the seemingly undesirable and the sinners who have believed like the first son will acquire salvation and that those who do not afterward repent will not. The first son was a sinner, perhaps, and might be seen as a sinner, but in repenting, he made himself right. The second son lied and did nothing. Jesus says that the tax collectors and sinners who believe will be with him but those seemingly righteous people who did not afterward repent and believe will not be in the kingdom of God.

The message here is found in answer to the question which son did the will of his father. It is clear that it was the repentant sinner who did and the lying, unbelieving son who did nothing and thus showed no love for his father and did not believe. Jesus concludes this parable with a statement that the tax collectors and undesirable who believe will be with him and that those who saw him and what he did, when they do not repent and believe him, will not enter the kingdom of God.

Jesus seems to say here that the repentant sinner and the seemingly unrighteous will be in the kingdom of God, but the very righteous in the world who do not afterward repent of their actions and believe will not be with him in the kingdom of God. The first son, it is true, failed initially in refusing to go to the vineyard but then underwent a moral change and transformation. The second son in his actions showed no love and rendered no help. Jesus says that we will be judged by our lives and actions and that even though our lives are seemingly misplaced and wrong directed, repentance will bring us into his presence and those whose actions show no love, as was the action of the second son, are in danger of condemnation, if not of being cut off in loneliness and isolation from the love of God and Christ.

Chapter 20
The Parable of the Great Supper

Matthew 22.1–11
And again Jesus spoke to them in parables, saying, "The kingdom of heaven may be compared to a king who gave a marriage feast for his son and sent his servants to call those who were invited to the marriage feast; but they would not come. Again he sent over other servants, saying, 'Tell those who are invited, Behold, I have made ready my dinner, my oxen and my fat calves are killed, and everything is ready. Come to the marriage feast.' But they made light of it and went off, one to his farm, another to his business, while the rest seized his servants, treated them shamefully, and killed them. The king was angry, and he sent his troops and destroyed those murderers and burned their city. Then he said to his servants, 'The wedding is ready, but those invited were not worthy. Go therefore to the thoroughfares, and invite to the marriage feast as many as you find.' And those servants went out into the streets and gathered all whom they found, both bad and good; so the wedding hall was filled with guests.

"But when the king came in to look at the guests, he saw there a man who had no wedding garment; and he said to him, 'Friend, how did you get in here without a wedding garment?' And he was speechless. Then the king said to the attendants, ' Bind him hand and foot, and cast into the outer darkness; there men will weep and gnash their teeth. For many are called, but few are chosen.'"

Luke 14.16–24
When one of those who sat at table with him heard this, he said to him, "Blessed is he who shall eat bread in the kingdom of God!" But he said to him, "A man once gave a great banquet, and invited many; and at the time for the banquet he sent his servant to say to those who had been invited, 'Come; for all is now ready.' But they all alike began to make excuses. The first said to him, 'I have bought a field, and I must go out and see it; I pray you, have me excused.' And an-

other said, 'I have brought five yoke of oxen, and I go to examine them. I pray you, have me excused.' And another said, 'I have married a wife, and therefore I cannot come.' So the servant came and reported this to his master. Then the householder in anger said to his servant, 'Go out quickly to the streets and lanes of the city, and bring in the poor and maimed and blind and lame.' And the servant said, 'Sir, what you commanded has been done, and still there is room.' And the master said to the servant, 'Go out to the highways and hedges, and compel people to come in, that my house may be filled. For I tell you, none of those men who were invited shall taste my banquet."

Both in Matthew and Luke, Matthew 22.1–10 and Luke 14.16–24, Jesus gives to us the Parable of the Great Supper. In this parable, he says that the kingdom of heaven can be compared to a king who gave a marriage feast for his son and sent his servants to call those who were invited to the marriage feast but they would not come. Again, he sent other servants saying to them to tell those who were invited since he had made ready his dinner and the marriage feast was completely ready. The persons who were invited by the servant apparently made fun of this invitation and went off, one to his farm, another to his business, while the rest seized his servants, treated them shamefully, and killed them. For this, the king was angry and he sent his troops and destroyed those murderers and burned their city. The king then said to his servants that the wedding was ready but those who were invited were not worthy. He told his servants to go to the streets and invite to the marriage feast as many as they could find. Those servants went out to these streets and gathered all whom they could find both good and bad. So, the wedding hall was filled with guests.

This is the narrative of the parable in Matthew 22.1–10. In Luke 14.16–24 the relation by Jesus of the parable is slightly different. Jesus says that a man gave a great banquet and invited many and said to those who had been invited that everything was ready but they all began to make excuses such as having bought a field and having to go out and see it, having bought five yoke of oxen and having to go examine them. while another said he had just married and could not come. The servant came and reported this to his master and the householder said to his servant to go out quickly to the streets and lanes of the city and bring in the poor, the maimed, the blind, and lame. The servant replied, "I have done what you commanded and there is still room." The master then said to his servant to go out to the highways and hedges and compel people to come in so that his house might be filled. The parable in Luke ends with a sentence, "I tell you none of those men invited shall taste my banquet."

The narrative in Luke is slightly different from that in Matthew in that various excuses are given. The householder tells his servant to go and bring in the poor, maimed , blind, and lame. The narrative in Matthew tells us that the servants were killed and that the king in his anger sent his troops to destroy the murderers and destroy their city. Again, the servant goes out to the streets and invites to the marriage feast both bad and good since those invited were not worthy, Matthew tells us.

This parable is fairly clear. The idea here is that in a sense the wedding feast and banquet is heaven itself: having a relationship of love with God and the guests at the banquet. The ability to understand this parable revolves around the concept and idea of an invitation by God. It is up to us whether we have the intellect and insight to respond to this invitation. Many in the world reject this invitation, not even to the level of indifference but to the point of active hostility toward God in Christ who extends this invitation to all of humanity with no strings attached.

In Matthew the invited guests not only declined to go but killed the servants who were extending the invitation. Matthew says that the invited were unworthy and both in Matthew and Luke we are provided with the great insight that the guests of God and Christ will not be whom we may expect. They may be the poor, the lamed, and the blind, and virtually anyone. In Matthew, we are told that the people who will receive and inhabit the kingdom of heaven in which this feast is assigned could be anyone and everyone.

Jesus tells us in this parable that the people who will be with him may not be the people whom the world honors and values but in fact the people who have the least value in the eyes of the world. Perhaps, Jesus tells us in this parable not to make outer judgments since his judgments like an x-ray pierce the souls and being of each of us. Who will be invited to the heavenly feast only may not be what we expect but in fact may not include us at all. The criteria for entrance into the kingdom of heaven and the heavenly feast are quite different for what we may have thought and may exclude the people whom the world and ourselves lay value on and include the degraded, the poverty stricken, and the most unattractive. In short, Jesus tells us the people who will be invited to the kingdom of heaven and to the heavenly feast may be those we least expect to be there and it is to those to whom Jesus extends his invitation of love for reasons unknown to replace those who seriously reject his claim and invitation.

It is not surprising that all of us continually turn down the good for something else. If the man who loves is not sufficiently wealthy, he is liable to be rejected by the woman he loves. Throughout world history, there has been a continual battle between good and evil which continues to this day. Good people rarely obtain political power and are for the most part excluded. There is an attraction to raw power which people grab on to and thus we have the Hitlers, Stalins, and Genghis Khans. For every man in prison there is a woman who decidedly and definitively loves him. The good is rejected and the bad are taken and accepted by many and all. Many people would rather have an expensive car than hear a great work of music which may cost them nothing. The people who will be at the heavenly feast will be those who we may not know God but whom God already knows and has found in the streets, byways, and alleys of the street.

Chapter 21
The Parable of the Guest Without a Wedding Garment

Matthew 22.11–14
"But when the king came in to look at the guests, he saw there a man who had no wedding garment; and he said to him, 'Friend, how did you get in here without a wedding garment?' And he was speechless. Then the king said to the attendants, 'Bind him hand and foot, and cast him into the outer darkness; there men will weep and gnash their teeth.' For many are called, but few are chosen."

In Matthew 22.11–14 Jesus gives us a very harsh message which many may find disturbing and inexplicable. In this parable the king comes in to look at the guest and sees there a man who has no wedding garment and says to him, "Friend, how did you get in here without a wedding garment?" The man is speechless and the king says to the attendants, "Bind this man hand and foot and cast him into the outer darkness where men will weep and gnash their teeth." The parable ends with an outstanding and emotionally disturbing statement that many are called but few are chosen.

It is hard to understand this parable here as to why not having a wedding garment results in virtual condemnation. The persons who was without a wedding garment had no inkling of the profundity and seriousness of the event which means having a relationship with God and Christ at the wedding. The person without the proper wedding garment has no respect or any idea of what the meaning is of having an encounter with God and Christ the King. Thus, the parable teaches us that when we come into the presence of God we must be prepared.

Still, the idea that not being ready for the occasion should result in a condemnation to what appears to be some sort of hell environment is hard to understand. Perhaps, the proper interpretation is that if we have not lived our lives being ready morally and spiritually for the heavenly banquet and wedding, we will be condemned. All of us are given the chance in the timeline of our lives to be ready on the basis of how we have lived in relationship to our neighbor.

Equally disturbing is the last sentence which says many are called but few are chosen. Perhaps, the best way to explain this last sentence is to understand that all of us as we live our lives are summoned and called, if you will, by God in Christ to form our lives and shape our lives into the potential humanity that God in creating us and calling us in Christ believes we are capable of. He extends his Eternal love and mercy to all humanity, but he tells us in this last sentence that although many are extended the invitation, few are chosen, ultimately. Perhaps, we can understand this last sentence as saying that if we look at ourselves and our selfish egotistical lives we may understand that although we may be called as all men and women are called by God, we will not be chosen not because God does not want us but because we have made the choice in our lives, as we have lived our lives not to be chosen.

The parable here says that we must be ready at all times for the ultimate encounter with Christ. If we are not ready, the consequences can and will be of utmost seriousness. The parable tells us that if we have not been made ready in our lives, we face eternal suffering. The parable also tells us that despite God's wish and desire to have relationship of love and joy with us all as his created beings that few will be found because their choices in their lives will make his choice of them impossible. In short, Jesus tells us the way we live our lives predetermines the ultimate outcome and that many will have made the eternal mistake which will result in something so hideous and terrible that we cannot even envision what eternal suffering forever might mean. The parable tells us that we will be cast somewhere in utter isolation and loneliness where we will be sad and grieved and unhappy for not taking the chance and opportunity that was offered to us in our lives by Christ. The parable tells us that many of us, if not most of us, will make this mistake, and Jesus tells us that this mistake will be horrendous for eternity.

Chapter 22
The Parable of the Burglar

Matthew 24.43-44
"But know this, that if the householder had known in what part of the night the thief was coming, he would have watched and would not have let his house be broken into. Therefore you also must be ready; for the Son of Man is coming at an hour you do not expect."

Luke 12.39-40
But know this, that if the householder had known at what hour the thief was coming, he would not have left his house to be broken into. You also must be ready; for the Son of man is coming at an unexpected hour."

The Parable of the Burglar is found in Matthew 24.43-44 and Luke 12. 39-40. In this parable as related in Matthew, Jesus tells us that if the householder had known what part of the night the thief was coming he would have watched and not have let his house be broken into. The parable ends in a sentence saying you must be ready because the Son of Man is coming and at an hour you do not expect.

In this parable Jesus uses the event of an occurrence such as a burglary to tell us of the imminent danger we face. He cautions us not to be unprepared like the householder, warning us that we do not know when the Son of Man may be coming and at an hour we may not expect.

The parable is somewhat peculiar in its structure since it analogizes the event of the coming of Christ and his return to a burglary. The coming of Christ should be an event of unbounded joy and happiness but Jesus uses the concept of a burglary and a thief breaking into someone's house as the image of the return of Christ.

I think what Jesus means here is that we cannot know exactly when Christ will come to us. The analogy is not that the coming of Christ is preceded by a criminal event but that we do not know when he will return, in what part of the night he will return, and we should be watchful, not unprepared. The idea is not that the return is like a burglary but that we do not know when he will come, and therefore we should be watchful and ready. The hour when Christ will return we cannot expect. If the householder had been watchful the thief would not have broken into his house. In the same way we must be ready.

It is the readiness and unexpectedness that are the key to understanding this parable. The parable tells us that we cannot know when Christ will return but we must always be ready. To be sure, to analogize preparedness to preventing a burglary is somewhat inexplicable. However, the message of the parable is readiness and the fact that we do not know when Christ will come to us and call us into account for our lives.

Chapter 23
The Parable of the Servant Entrusted with Supervision

Matthew 24.45–51
"Who then is the faithful and wise servant, whom his master has set over his household to give them their food at the proper time? Blessed is that servant whom his master when he comes will find so doing. Truly, I say to you he will set him over all his possessions. But if that wicked servant says to himself, 'My master is delayed,' and begins to beat his fellow servants and eats and drinks with the drunken, the master of that servant will come on a day when he does not expect him and will punish him and put him with the hypocrites; there men will weep and gnash their teeth."

Luke 12.42-46
And the Lord said, "Who then is the faithful and wise steward, whom his master will set over his household, to give them their portion of food at the proper time? Blessed is that servant whom when he comes will find so doing. Truly, I say to you, he will set him over all his possessions. But if that servant says to himself, 'My master is delayed in coming,' and begins to beat the menservants and to eat and drink and get drunk, the master of that servant will come on a day when he does not expect him and at an hour he does not know and will punish him and put him with the unfaithful."

This parable is found in Matthew 24.45–51 and Luke 12.42-46. In Matthew 24, Jesus tells us that the servant is faithful and wise who, when his master comes, he finds him giving food at the proper time. Jesus says that the master will set that servant over all his possessions. Matthew then says that if the wicked servant says, "My master is delayed," and begins to beat his fellow servants and eats and drinks with the drunken, the master will come on a day when he does not expect him and will punish him and put him with the hypocrites where men will weep and gnash their teeth. The version in Luke is slightly different in that Luke ends with the sentence that the master of the servant who beats his fellow servants and eats and drink and gets drunk will come on a day when he does not expect him and at an hour he does not know and will punish him and put him with the unfaithful.

In this parable, the servant is placed in a situation of supervision over the household while his master is delayed. The issue is whether the servant who is so entrusted will attack his fellow servants and eat and virtually get drunk. The parable ends both in Matthew and Luke with a warning that the master will return on a day the servant does not expect and at an hour he does not know and will punish him where men, so Matthew says, will weep and gnash their teeth, and in Luke, will punish him and put him with the unfaithful.

This is a parable of warning to all of us. All of us are in positions of trust with respect to others, our families, and if you will, ourselves. This position of trust is significant and Jesus warns us that if we fail in our lives in this way to those over whom we are put in power and with whom we are entrusted we will be punished. If we abuse that trust and abuse our power over others whose lives and wellbeing are entrusted to us, we will be punished and condemned, and it would appear we would be placed in some sort of eternal punishment. Matthew says we will be placed with the hypocrites and Luke says we will be placed with the unfaithful.

The meaning and content of this parable is, I think, clear. All of us in our lives are placed in positions of trust with respect to others. This position could be a position of trust over family members, over people we work with, over the neighbors in our community, or virtually anyone with whom we may have to deal. In some way, Jesus tells us in this parable that we are in a position of trust with everyone we encounter and with everyone with whom we have a relationship in our lives. If we abuse that trust we will not be forgiven but will be cast into condemnation from which there will be no escape.

In our lives, we have the chance to be people who are worthy of trust and who can be trusted with others and literally with whomever we may encounter. In short, Jesus tells us that we are all given a chance to be what we should be in relation to the trust with which we are placed over others.

In some sense we have a position of trust over everyone and anyone we encounter in our lives. The doctor whose sole aim is money and wealth and abuses his obligation as a doctor to cure and make less money in doing so has abused his position of trust. The lawyer who charges unduly for little or no work on behalf of his client has abused his position of trust. The mother or father who passes on no values but egotism, selfishness, and greed to their children have abused their position of trust. The auto mechanic who, rather than finding the simple answer to a mechanical problem, says to the customer that a new transmission and brakes are needed has abused his position of trust. The priest or minister who does not tell his congregation about Jesus Christ and his claim to offer eternal life has abused his position of trust. The person who does not exercise love and kindness and help to his neighbor has
abused his position of trust.

In short, every one of us is in a position of trust with everyone else. Jesus tells us that should we abuse throughout our lives the trust with which God himself has entrusted us, we will suffer the consequences of eternal death and suffering.

Chapter 24
The Parable of the Ten Virgins

Matthew 25.1–13
"Then the kingdom of heaven shall be compared to ten maidens who took their lamps and went to meet the bridegroom. Five of them were foolish, and five were wise. For when the foolish took their lamps, they took no oil with them; but the wise took flasks of oil with their lamps. As the bridegroom was delayed, they all slumbered and slept. But at midnight there was a cry, 'Behold, the bridegroom! Come out to meet him.' Then all those maidens rose and trimmed their lamps. And the foolish said to the wise, 'Give us some of your oil, for our lamps are going out.' But the wise replied, 'Perhaps there will not be enough for us and for you; go rather to the dealers and buy for yourselves.' And while they went to buy, the bridegroom came and those who were ready went in with him to the marriage feast; and the door was shut. Afterward the other maidens came also, saying, 'Lord, lord, open to us.' But he replied, 'Truly, I say to you, I do not know you.' Watch therefore, for you know neither the day nor the hour."

This parable is one of the most familiar told and related by Jesus in the Gospel of Matthew. In this parable, Jesus compares the kingdom of heaven to ten maidens who took their lamps and went to meet the bridegroom. Five of them were said to be foolish and five wise because when the foolish took their lamps they took no oil with them, but the wise took flasks of oil with their lamps. While the bridegroom was delayed they slept, but at midnight there was a cry that the bridegroom had arrived and they should come out and meet him.

Then all the maidens arose and trimmed their lamps. The foolish wanted the wise to give the foolish some of their oil because the lamps of the foolish were going out. The wise replied that there would not be enough for both groups and advised the foolish to go to the dealers and buy oil for themselves. While the foolish went out to buy, the bridegroom came. Those who were ready went with him to the marriage feast and the door was shut. Afterwards the other maidens came saying, "Lord, Lord, open to us." The parable ends with the sentences, "I do not know you." "Watch therefore for you know neither the day nor the hour."

This parable may be seen as an allegory of the coming of Christ. Christ is the bridegroom and the ten virgins are those people, Christians, who are awaiting his coming. The idea behind the parable is that we must be prepared, that is be expectant Christians, for the coming of Christ. Those who in their lives are ready for his coming are welcomed to the heavenly feast. Those who are too late in preparation in their lives are excluded from the heavenly banquet.

Those who in their lives do not live their lives in Christ and are not ready when he comes will be told that he does not know them. The ultimate admonition is to keep alert and watch, for none of us knows the day or the hour we will be summoned to be with Christ. In short, I think this parable should be seen as an allegory of the coming of Christ and the fact that we must be ready at all times, since we in the Christian community or, better put as individual Christians, will never know when he will come and welcome us to his presence. If we have not been ready morally and spiritually in our lives to that point, then we will not be ready, and not being ready we will not be welcomed to share in the joy and happiness in eternal life with Christ in the world and days to come.

Chapter 25
The Parable of the Pounds and Talents

Matthew 25.14–30
"For it will be as when a man going on a journey called his servants and entrusted to them his property; to one he gave five talents, to another two, to another one, to each according to his ability. Then he went away. He who had received the five talents went at once and traded with them; and he made five talents more. So also, he who had the two talents made two talents more. But he who had received the one talent went and dug in the ground and hid his master's money.

"Now after a long time the master of those servants came and settled accounts with them. And he who had received the five talents came forward, bringing five talents more, saying, 'Master you delivered to me five talents; here I have made five talents more.' His master said to him, 'Well done, good and faithful servant; you have been faithful over a little, I will set you over much; enter into the joy of your master.'

"And he also who had the two talents came forward, saying, 'Master, you delivered to me two talents; here I have made two talents more.' His master said to him, 'Well done, good and faithful servant. You have been faithful over a little, I will set you over much; enter into the joy of your master.'

"He also who had received the one talent came forward, saying, 'Master, I knew you to be a hard man, reaping where you did not sow, and gathering where you did not winnow; so I was afraid, and I went and hid your talent in the ground. Here you have what is yours.' But his master answered him, 'You wicked and slothful servant! You knew that I reap where I have not winnowed? Then you ought to have invested my money with the bankers, and at my coming I should have received what was my own with interest. So take the talent from him, and give it to him who has the ten talents. For to everyone who has, will more be given, and he will have abundance; but from him who has not, even what he has will be taken away. And cast the worthless servant into the outer darkness; there men will weep and gnash their teeth.'"

Luke 19.12–27

He said therefore, "A nobleman went into a far country to receive a kingdom and then return. Calling ten of his servants, he gave them ten pounds, and said to them, 'Trade with these till I come.' But his citizens hated him and sent an embassy after him, saying, 'We do not want this man to reign over us.' When he returned, having received the kingdom, he commanded these servants, to whom he had given the money, to be called to him that he might know what they had gained by trading. The first came before him, saying, 'Lord, your pound has made ten pounds more.' And he said to him, 'Well done, good servant! Because you have been faithful in a very little, you shall have authority over ten cities.' And the second came, saying, 'Lord, your pound has made five pounds.' And he said to him, 'And you are to be over five cities.' Then another came, saying, 'Lord, here is your pound, which I kept laid away in a napkin; for I was afraid of you, because you are a severe man; you take up what you did not lay down, and reap what you did not sow.' He said to him, 'I will condemn you out of your own mouth, you wicked servant! You knew that I was a severe man, taking up what I did not lay down and reaping what I did not sow? Why then did you not put my money into the bank, and at my coming I should have collected it with interest?' And he said to those who stood by, 'Take the pound from him, and give it to him who has the ten pounds.' (And they said to him, 'Lord, he has ten pounds!') 'I tell you, that to everyone who has, will more be given; but from him who has not, even what he has will be taken away. But as for these enemies of mine, who did not want me to reign over them, bring them here and slay them before me.'"

The Parable of the Pounds and Talents is related in Matthew 25.14–30 and Luke 19.12–27. In Matthew, the parable as related by Jesus is that when a man was going on a journey, he called his servants and entrusted to them his property, giving to one five talents, to another two talents, and to another one talent, each according to his ability. When the man went away, the servant who received the five talents traded with them and made five talents more, as did the one who had two talents. The one who had received the one talent dug and hid that one talent in the ground. The master then returned and the one who had received five talents told the master that he had made five talents more, and the master complimented him saying, "Well done good and faithful servant; you have been faithful over a little. I will set you over much" and "Enter into the joy of your master." The same thing happened with the servant who was entrusted with two talents, who said to the master he had made two talents more, and his master said to him, "Well done, I will set you over much" and "Enter into the joy of your master." The servant who had received one talent said to the master that he knew him to be a hard person and had been afraid so he went and hid the talent in the ground and presented it now. The master answered him, "You wicked and slothful servant," saying to him, "You ought to have invested my money with the bankers and at my coming I should have received what was my own with interest." The master took the talent from him and gave it to the servant who had the ten talents stating that to everyone who has, more will be more given but from him who has not, even what he has will be taken away. The parable concludes in Matthew with a sentence that the worthless servant is cast into outer darkness.

The narrative in Luke Chapter 19 is slightly different. In Luke Jesus says that a nobleman went into a far country to receive a kingdom. He had called ten of his servants and had given them ten pounds, saying to them, "Trade with these until I return." However, Luke says that the citizens hated these servants and sent an embassy to the noblemen saying, "We do not want these servants to reign over us." The nobleman returned, having received the kingdom, and asked the servants what they had gained by trading. The first came and said that he had made ten pounds more, and the master said, "Well done and you shall have authority over ten cities." The second one said that he had made five pounds more and the master gave him authority over five cities. The third servant said that he hidden the money in a napkin. The master then said that he would condemn the servant who admitted knowing the master was a severe man and he asked why the man did not put the money into the bank. The master then said to those who stood by, "Take the pound from him and give it to the servant who has ten pounds."

The conclusion to Matthew is slightly different but its thrust is the same: to those who have, more will be given, but to those who have not, that little will be taken away. Thus, the differences between Matthew and Luke are fairly obvious. In Luke there is a nobleman who goes on a journey to claim a kingdom. In Matthew there is a merchant who goes on a journey. In Luke a deputation or embassy is sent after the nobleman indicating their unhappiness with these servants who were reigning over them. In Luke the nobleman returns as a king. In Luke verse 27, the enemies who did not want the nobleman to rule over them are murdered and slain. In Luke, one of the servants hid the money in a napkin, a variant reading that is not present in Matthew where the servant is said to have dug a hole in the ground and hidden the money.

Other than these small differences, the narratives in both Matthew and Luke are fairly consistent. This parable is somewhat difficult to understand. I would like to suggest a possible interpretation and give my thoughts. Jesus seems to be saying here that just as these servants were given differing amounts of money in connection with their ability as persons, we are all not equal in our abilities and have different abilities but that we in our lives must make full and adequate use of our talents and abilities. To put it better, we must make the best of it.

Another aspect of the parable that is important is that we must try and that the servant who did nothing with the talent he was entrusted with is worthy of condemnation apparently. The world is composed of many different kinds of people of varying talents and abilities, some with more and some with less. Jesus tells us here that if we do nothing with whatever talents we had been given as persons in our lives, we will lose out entirely, but to those who make great effort as much as they can do, not only will they be rewarded but will be given more than others, even in abundance. As for the person who makes no effort in his time that he has been given, even what he has as a person will be taken from him. In Matthew, Jesus says that he will be condemned to what appears to be some sort of hell.

Jesus seems to be saying in this parable that God gives everybody something of a chance to do something with their lives. Jesus well knows that people are varying in their talents and abilities and does not say that everybody has equal talents and abilities. He does say that whatever we have been given we must make use of and not stand by idly, perhaps envying the people who had been given more than us. There is something of a condemnation here of laziness and of not trying to do something with our lives that God has given to us. This is the best I can say of what the parable means.

In my own experience, I myself realize that I have some talents and perhaps some other limited talents and abilities, but I realize that I must try to do my part in the world. Jesus says that those who do not take that route are unworthy in his eyes. In Matthew, he says, "They will be cast into outer darkness where men will weep and gnash their teeth." Luke says, as in Matthew, that for the person who did nothing with what they had in their lives, whatever they have will be removed from them. Jesus says that in the case of the person who makes no effort with the little they have in their lives, even that will be taken from them and they will be left with nothing.

Chapter 26
The Parable of the Last Judgment

Matthew 25.31–46
"When the Son of Man comes in his glory and all the angels with him, then he will sit on his glorious throne. Before him will be gathered all the nations, and he will separate them one from another as a shepherd separates the sheep from the goats, and he will place the sheep at his right hand, but the goats at the left. Then the King will say to those at his right hand, 'Come, O blessed of my father, inherit the kingdom prepared for you from the foundation of the world; for I was hungry and you gave me food, I was thirsty and you gave me drink, I was a stranger and you welcomed me, I was naked and you clothed me, I was sick and you visited me, I was in prison and you came to me.' Then the righteous will answer him, 'Lord, when did we see thee hungry and feed thee, or thirsty and give thee drink? And when did we see thee a stranger and welcome thee, or naked and clothe thee? And when did we see thee sick or in prison and visit thee?' And the King will answer them, 'Truly, I say to you, as you did it to one of the least of these my brethren, you did it to me.' Then he will say to those at his left hand, 'Depart from me, you cursed, into the eternal fire prepared for the devil and his angels; for I was hungry and you gave me no food, I was thirsty and you gave me no drink, I was a stranger and you did not clothe me, sick and in prison and you did not visit me.' Then they also will answer, 'Lord, when did we see thee hungry or thirsty or a stranger or naked or sick or in prison, and did not minister to thee?' Then he will answer to them, 'Truly, I say to you, as you did it not to one of the least of these, you did it not to me.' And they will go away into eternal punishment, but the righteous into eternal life."

The Parable of the Last Judgment is found in Matthew Chapter 25.31–46. In this parable, Jesus says that when he comes back in glory with the angels with him, he will sit on his glorious throne and before him will be gathered all nations and he will separate them, as a shepherd separates the sheep from the goats, and place the sheep on his right hand but the goats on his left. Then the king will say to those on his right, "Come and inherit the kingdom, for I was hungry and you gave me food; I was thirsty and you gave me drink; I was a stranger and you welcomed me; I was naked and you clothed me; I was sick and you visited me; and I was imprisoned and you came to me." There follow the sentences that the righteous will answer Christ, "When did we see you hungry and feed you or thirsty and give you drink? When did we see you as a stranger or naked and clothe you? When did we see you sick or imprisoned and visit you?" The king will then answer that truly as you did to the least of these you did to me.

The king will then say to those at his left hand, "Depart from me, you cursed, into the eternal fire prepared for the devil and his angels for I was hungry and you gave me no food; I was thirsty and you gave me no drink; I was a stranger and you did not clothe me; sick and imprisoned and you did not visit me." Jesus then says that they will answer, "Lord when did we see you hungry or thirsty or a stranger or naked or sick or imprisoned, and did not minister to you?" The king will then answer, "What you did not to the least of these you did not to me and you will go away into eternal punishment but the righteous into eternal life?"

The thrust of this parable is first that there will be a last judgment when Jesus will return in glory with all the angels and will sit on his glorious throne and will make a judgment on all people and nations separating one from the other, one group to be in heaven—the righteous—the other, to be condemned in eternal punishment in hell. That is the first point of the parable.

The second point is what the criteria will be for the judgment that will be made on all men and women. At first glance Jesus tells us that those persons will be accounted righteous and saved who gave him food when hungry, gave him drink when he was thirsty, welcomed him when a stranger, clothed him when naked, visited him when sick, and came to him in prison. The righteous then raise the issue that they never saw these particular scenarios, whether the king being hungry or thirsty or naked or sick or imprisoned. The answer of Christ at that point is that the criterion is how you treated the least of persons in your life. It is the least significant and impoverished people whom: if you see hungry you do not feed them, whom you see thirsty and do not give them drink, whom you do not welcome as a stranger, whom you do not give clothes if naked, or visit when sick or imprisoned, it is as if you are doing this to Christ himself. Jesus says what you do to the least person in your life, you take a stab at him.

Then there is the point made that the unrighteous will say they never saw Christ hungry or thirsty or a stranger naked or imprisoned or sick and did not then minister to him. Again, Jesus provides the answer, what you do to anyone, even the least person in this life, you do to him.

The righteous are answered with the same answer. To the question they ask about whether they saw the conditions that Jesus described of hunger, thirst, sickness and imprisonment, and nakedness. The righteous asked when they saw Christ like this. Jesus answers, "What you do to the least of persons in this life, you did to me."

To the evildoers who are condemned that they never saw the things Christ describes here, the answer is, "You never gave the help at any time to the least and in not doing so you did it to me."

In short, the point of the parable is that there will be a last judgment and the judgment will not be based on verbal professions that they did their part for Christ in God but on the treatment they gave the least in this world whom if they were hungry gave them food, if they were thirsty gave them drink, if they were strangers clothed them, and sick and imprisoned visited them. Jesus tells us that at the last judgment in the end, the criteria for judgment will not be how we treated our family, the people we like, the people that attract us, or the people who can do something for us, but how we treat the least desirable in society. The criteria for the last judgment will not be what verbal professions of faith we make but how we treat all others in the course of our lives and whether when we had the opportunity we took it. Jesus says that if we do not do the things we did in this parable but merely devote ourselves to ourselves and our families, we are in danger of eternal punishments and of condemnation into the eternal fire prepared for the devil and his angels.

There is a warning in this parable and the warning is clear. It is not enough to attend to our own affairs and possibly the affairs of our own family. Much more is demanded of us and the demand is that we fulfill the commandments and rules that Christ has outlined here. If we spend our lives entertaining ourselves, taking care of ourselves, the point of the parable of what may happen to us is eminently clear.

Chapter 27
The Parable of the Two Debtors

Luke 7.36–48
One of the Pharisees asked him to eat with him, and he went into the Pharisee's house, and took his place at table. And behold, a woman of the city, who was a sinner, when she learned that he was at table in the Pharisee's house brought an alabaster flask of ointment and standing behind him at his feet, weeping, she began to wet his feet with her tears and wiped them with the hair of her head and kissed his feet and anointed them with the ointment. Now when the Pharisee who had invited him saw it, he said to himself, "If this man were a prophet, he would have known who and what sort of woman this is who is touching him, for she is a sinner." And Jesus answering said to him, "Simon, I have something to say to you." And he answered, "What is it, Teacher?" "A certain creditor had two debtors; one owed five hundred denarii and the other fifty. When they could not pay, he forgave them both. Now which of them will love him more?" Simon answered, "The one, I suppose, to whom he forgave more." And he said to him, "You have judged rightly." Then turning toward the woman he said to Simon, "Do you see this woman? I entered your house, you gave me no water for my feet, but she has wet my feet with her tears and wiped them with her hair. You gave me no kiss, but from the time I came in she has not ceased to kiss my feet. You did not anoint my head with oil, but she has anointed my feet with ointment. Therefore I tell you, her sins, which are many, are forgiven, for she loved much; but he who is forgiven little, loves little." And he said to her, "Your sins are forgiven."

This parable is preceded with a discussion which begins with a statement that one of the Pharisees asked Jesus to eat with him and a woman of the city, who was a sinner, perhaps a prostitute, when she learned that Jesus was at table at the Pharisees house, brought a flask of ointment and standing behind him at his feet, weeping, she began to wet his feet with her tears and wipe them with the hair of her head, kissed his feet, and anointed them with the ointment. The Pharisee stated that if Jesus were a prophet he would have known what sort of
woman this was who was touching him, since she was a sinner. Jesus answered

the following, saying there was a certain creditor who had two debtors: one who owed him five-hundred denarii and the other fifty. When they could not pay he forgave them both. Jesus asked of Simon who would love him more and Simon answered, "The one whom he forgave more." Turning to the woman, Jesus said to Simon, that he gave him no water for his feet but the woman wet his feet with her tears, kissed his feet, and wiped his feet with her hair. Jesus said that Simon gave him no water for his feet, did not anoint his head with oil, but the woman anointed his feet with ointment. Jesus concludes with the statement that the woman's sins are forgiven for her great love, for he who is forgiven little, loves little.

Apparently, the parable begins with a banquet to which Jesus was invited. Simon may have regarded Jesus as a prophet. The undesirability attached to the woman either indicated that she was a prostitute or engaged in some dishonorable activity. The woman is shown as weeping and wetting Jesus' feet with her tears, wiping them with her hair, kissing his feet, and anointing his feet with ointment. These actions indicates the woman's great love and, as it were, recognition of Jesus as the Savior. It is not clear what prompted the woman's actions but they are the display of great thankfulness.

Simon raises the issue of why Jesus lets a sinner touch him. The actions of the woman here are actions of love. The woman's love is so great that she loosens her hair in public, weeps, and wipes Jesus' feet with her long hair. These actions indicate a person who has given up all sense of modesty and potential embarrassment in her love for Christ. Kissing the Savior's feet is evidence of her great love. Simon is shocked at Jesus' allowing this sinner to do this. This is one part of the parable.

Jesus perhaps is telling us that a sinner, a woman of ill repute, has greater sensitivity and understanding so that in the presence of Jesus she is drawn to him with great love and is literally wiping his feet with oil and kissing his feet and wiping it with her hair. Can anything show that this sinner recognized who Jesus was, perhaps more than the great and important of the world? More importantly, Simon, the Pharisee, did nothing approaching these sort of actions, but in fact in his world, a person of Jesus' stature would have nothing to do with a woman of this background to approach him, let alone touch him in the fashion she did. For Simon, the Pharisee, his religious world is one of hierarchy, where the religious great are at the top and a woman of this sort is literally unwelcome and certainly untouchable. Jesus is informing Simon, the Pharisee, otherwise and telling him where true love and greatness lie.

Jesus goes on to explain about the two debtors, concluding that the one whose debt was great, whom he forgave, will love him more, since his action showed a greater love than the other person's. Jesus then points out what the women did to exhibit her great love and contrasts it with Simon's actions. This shows her great love and for her great love, her sins are forgiven.

Then, Jesus concludes with the statement that the little love that we give to people will result in little forgiveness. Jesus tells us here that the key is love and great love. Forgiving the great debt is an act of great love and the response will be great love. Simon exhibited little love and the woman who showed great love despite her many sins was forgiven, but Jesus then concludes with a statement, reversing the tables and thinking, "He who forgives little, loves little," thereby equating forgiveness with love. This is a third point that Jesus makes in the parable.

Chapter 28
The Parable of the Good Samaritan

Luke 10.25-37
And behold, a lawyer stood up to put him to the test, saying, "Teacher, what shall I do to inherit eternal life?" He said to him, "What is written in the law? How do you read?" And he answered, "You shall love the Lord your God with all your heart, and with all your soul, and with all your strength, and with all your mind; and your neighbor as yourself." And he said to him, "You have answered right; do this, and you will live." But he, desiring to justify himself, said to Jesus, "And who is my neighbor?" Jesus replied, "A man was going down from Jerusalem to Jericho, and he fell among robbers, who stripped him and beat him, and departed, leaving him half dead. Now by chance a priest was going down that road; and when he saw him he passed by on the other side. So likewise a Levite, when he came to the place and saw him, passed by on the other side. But a Samaritan, as he journeyed, came to where he was; and when he saw him, he had compassion and went to him and bound up his wounds, pouring oil and wine; then he set him on his own beast and brought him to an inn, and took care of him. And the next day he took out two denarii and gave them to the innkeeper, saying, 'Take care of him; and whatever more you spend, I will repay you when I come back.' Which of these three, do you think, proved neighbor to the man who fell among the robbers?" He said, "The one who showed mercy on him." And Jesus said to him, "Go and do likewise."

The Parable of the Good Samaritan is one of the most familiar to most of us. The story begins in Luke, Chapter 10, with the question put by a lawyer as to what he should do to inherit eternal life. Jesus tells him that the Law commands that you love the Lord with all your heart, soul, strength, and mind. If he did this, he would live. The lawyer then asks who his neighbor is, and Jesus tells the story of the Good Samaritan. The story is familiar to many, but in short, Jesus says that a man was going down from Jerusalem to Jericho, fell among robbers, who stripped him, beat him, and departed, leaving him half dead. Jesus then says a priest was going down that road, and when he saw him, he passed down on the other side. Jesus then says a Levite, when he came down to the same place and saw him, passed down on the other side. Jesus then says that a Samaritan, as he journeyed, came to where the injured man was and when he saw him, he had compassion and went to him and bound up his wounds, pouring oil and wine, and then set him on his own beast and brought him to an inn and took care of him. The next day he took out two denarii and gave them to the innkeeper saying, "Take care of him and whatever more you spend I will repay you, when I come back." Jesus asks the question, "Which of the three do you think proved neighbor to the man who fell among the robbers." The answer of the lawyer is, "The one who showed mercy on him." Jesus says to him, "Go and do likewise."

This parable has two significant thought streams. The first is that we cannot judge people by their societal status and titles, even their religious titles. We cannot make a judgment on a person because they are a priest, or Levite. Jesus tells us that the person is to be judged individually, and on their own actions. In this particular parable, the high status religious leader showed no mercy in passing this wounded person stripped, beaten, and half dead. Both the Levite and the priest not only passed by, but passed by on the other side. We are then told that the societal outcast of the time, a Samaritan, came to where this person lay suffering and had compassion and showed mercy.

Samaritans were outcast to the Jewish community, virtually nonpersons. They occupied the similar position that a black man in America might have occupied in the late 19th century and early 20th century. African Americans at that time had few educational opportunities, few or little economic or job opportunities, and at least in the South, were kept in an underclass status, and in fact, until the 1950s, were the subject and object of beatings and lynchings. Thus, when Jesus says in this parable that it was the outcast underclass person who not only showed compassion, went to the person, bound up his wound, set him up on his beast, brought him to an inn, took care of him, and gave the innkeeper additional money to take care of the person, he is telling us who the true neighbor is. More significantly, he tells us that the judgments of society and the world on persons is misguided and incorrect.

It was the outcast in this parable and undesirable who was the neighbor, and showed great love, mercy, and compassion. The Levite and the priest, despite their outward religious professions, had no compassion and no mercy. The societally undesirably person exhibited those qualities.

Thus, one can find a number of points in this parable, namely, that our neighbor is the person who exhibits love and compassion in relation to us, wherever that person may be found, and whatever occasion or situation we are cast in with him. Two: that the world's evaluation system on status, titles, and money are twisted and incorrect and that a person is to be judged on the qualities that the Samaritan exhibited in this parable, whether that person is in rags, or in the gutter, or is a CEO in an office building on Wall Street.

Chapter 29
The Parable of the Friend Who Asked for Help

Luke 11.5-8
And he said to them, "Which of you who has a friend will go to him at midnight and say to him, 'Friend, lend me three loaves; for a friend of mine has arrived on a journey, and I have nothing to set before him'; and he will answer from within, 'Do not bother me; the door is now shut, and my children are with me in bed; I cannot get up and give you anything'? I tell you, though he will not get up and give him anything because he is this friend, yet because of this importunity he will rise and give him whatever he needs."

In this parable, Jesus tells us perhaps how we should relate to others and to him, as a person. He says in the parable, and exhorts us and asks us, to consider the following; he says, "Which of you, who has a friend, will go to him at midnight and ask to borrow three loaves of bread for a friend who has arrived on a journey," and he has had to tell the visitor, "I have nothing to set before you." Then Jesus says, that the person responds, "Do not bother me, the door is now shut, and my children are with me in bed, and I cannot get up to give you anything." Jesus concludes in this parable that although this person will not get up and give him anything, yet, because of his asking, and importunity, he will rise up and give him whatever he needs.

In this parable, Jesus represents the annoyance of the neighbor, being disturbed and annoyed, and the neighbor says to this request that his house is closed now and his children are in bed. Jesus tells us that because of this person's asking, the request is complied with. Perhaps in this parable, Jesus is advising us to always pray and never cease doing so, because nothing is impossible to be granted when we ask. In addition, the parable may be interpreted by the obligation not to refuse such a request. The neighbor is being asked for help and Jesus seems to tell us here that if we are the object and subject of such a request by another person, we should not refuse on the grounds of annoyance and inconvenience. If we do not grant the request of our neighbor for help for friendship's sake, we should at least do so because we are being asked for help.

In this parable we are told, number one, that God grants our petitions and prayers, if we persist; two, we should always ask; three, if our neighbor asks for help we have an obligation to provide it and hearken to his cry for help, even if it should annoy and inconvenience us, or we should have no inclination to be bothered by the entire scenario. In this parable, we are told that, as we hearken to the cry of the needy, God also will hearken to our cry when we are in need, and to all those in need,

In short, we are told here that God will listen to our cry when we are in need, if we ask, and two, in our lives, we must hearken to the cry of the needy however much it distresses us in our lives to be bothered. The key to this parable is one, that we must pray and petition constantly; two, that God will hearken to our cry in need; and three, we must hearken to the cry of the needy in our lives and not deny their request for help.

Chapter 30
The Parable of the Rich Fool

Luke 12. 16-21
And he told them a parable, saying, "The land of a rich man brought forth plentifully; and he thought to himself, 'What shall I do, for I have nowhere to store my crops?' And he said, 'I will do this: I will pull down my barns, and build larger ones; and there I will store all my grain and my goods. And I will say to my soul, Soul, you have ample goods laid up for many years; take your ease, east, drink, be merry.' But God said to him, 'Fool! This night your soul is required of you; and the things you have prepared, whose will they be?' So is he who lays up treasure for himself, and is not rich toward God."

In this parable, called the Parable of the Rich Fool, Jesus tells us that the land of a rich man brought forth plentifully and he thought to himself, "What shall I do? I have nowhere to store my crops." Jesus says that the man says, I will pull down my barns and build larger ones and there I will store all my grain and my goods. The man is then represented as saying to his soul, "You have ample goods laid up for many years, take your ease, eat, drink, and be merry." God then says to him, "Fool, this night your soul is required of you and the things you have prepared, whose they will be?" The conclusion of the parable is, "So is he who lays up treasure for himself, and is not rich toward God."

This parable presents some problems of interpretation. Essentially, the parable presents a view of a rich farmer who thinks he has no fear of a bad harvest and can simply take his ease, can simply build bigger barns with no fear of a bad harvest where he can store all his grain and goods. In fact, in this parable, Jesus warns us that this is a rich fool of a farmer since he has no fear of anything happening to him or, better put, thinks that he can have bigger and bigger harvests, can build a larger barn where he can store all his grain and goods, and having done so he can, so to speak, make merry and take his ease.

I think that Jesus says here that this rich fool does not understand that he is mortal and that we can be called by God out of this life at any time and, at that time, there will be a judgment, and that the goods that were prepared and stored up will do this person no good. Jesus concludes this parable by saying that those of us who solely layup treasure for themselves but fail to be rich toward God will have a consequence.

There are two messages in this parable. One is the misplaced confidence of the rich man in thinking that the harvest will always be plentiful and nothing can happen to him, and that he can eat drink and be merry forever. The second message of the parable is that Jesus tells us our soul can be required of us at any time, and the things we have kept for ourselves and thought would shield us from our essential mortality and the ultimate issue of death mortality and judgment by God, these will do us no good. Jesus tells us here that we should live our lives not laying up things for ourselves whatever they may be, whether material goods, riches, or honors, or whatever we set a value on for ourselves, but our lives should not be laying up those things to ourselves, but laying up and living our lives toward God and in God.

Chapter 31
The Parable of the Barren Fig Tree

Luke 13.6–9
And he told this parable: "A man had a fig tree planted in his vineyard; and he came seeking fruit on it and found none. And he said to the vinedresser, 'Lo, these three years I have come seeking fruit on this fig tree, and I find none. Cut it down; why should it use up the ground?' And he answered him, 'Let it alone, sir, this year also, till I dig about it and put manure on it. And if it bears fruit next year, well and good; but if not, you can cut it down.'"

The parable of the barren fig tree is one of the shorter parables that Jesus lies before his audience. The parable can be summarized as a man had a fig tree planted in his, vineyard, and he came seeking fruit, and found none, and he tells his vine dresser that for three years he had come seeking fruit on this fig tree and found none. He is represented further saying to the vine dresser, cut the fig tree down, why should it use up the ground, implying the fig tree was of no use, since it had bore no fruit for three years. The response of the vine dresser was to let the matter alone and let him dig about it and put on manure. The vine dresser says, if the tree bears fruit next year, that is fine, but if not, you can cut it down.

     This parable starts with the supposition or principle, that there should be permitted three years for the fig tree to grow. Hence, since that time had passed, and the fig tree was unsuccessful in bearing no fruit, the vine dresser proposes to give it another year with fertilizer or manure. This request is granted. It is not clear precisely how this parable is to be exactly interpreted. It is possible that the idea behind it is that we are given an added chance in our lives when we have done no good works or truly righteous actions, that God will give us a second chance. The idea is that there will be a stay of a possible judgment for life that is wasted, and that we will be given another chance by God to be what he wants us to be. When this limit has been passed, and nevertheless we are the same, there will be a final judgment, and God's mercy, which had been extended, will no longer be so. Perhaps the parable could represent a second chance for repentance or at least a change about or improvement. The parable seems to say that God will give us more time or added chance, to bear good fruit, or be the good person he would want us to be, but there will come a time when he will no longer give us any other chances and we will judge on the basis of our lives and works.

Chapter 32
The Parable of the Closed Door

Luke 13.24–30
"Strive to enter by the narrow door; for many, I tell you, will seek to enter and will not be able. When once the householder has risen up and shut the door, you will begin to stand outside and to knock at the door, saying, 'Lord, open to us.' He will answer you, 'I do not know where you come from.' Then you will begin to say, 'We ate and drank in your presence, and you taught in our streets.' But he will say, 'I tell you, I do not know where you come from; depart from me, all you workers of iniquity!' There you will weep and gnash you teeth when you see Abraham and Isaac and Jacob and all the prophets in the kingdom of God and you yourselves thrust out. And men will come from east and west, and from north and south, and sit at table in the kingdom of God. And behold, some are last who will be first, and some are first who will be last."

On the other hand, in the parable of the closed door, found in Luke 13:24–30, I think the thrust and meaning are very clear. Nevertheless, I would like to give some discussion and interpretation of this parable. In this parable, Jesus begins by saying we should strive to enter by the narrow door and adds that many will seek to enter and will not be able to. He then says, that when once the householder has risen up and shut the door, you will begin to stand outside and knock on the door saying, "Lord, open to us." The Lord will answer to this request, "I do not know where you came from," and you will respond, "We ate and drank in your presence and you taught in our streets." The Lord will then respond, "I tell you I do not know where you come from; depart from me, all you workers of iniquity." Jesus concludes with the statement that the Lord states, "There you will weep gnash your teeth, when you see Abraham and Isaac and Jacob, and all the prophets in the kingdom of God and you yourselves thrust out." The parable ends with a statement that men will come from east and west, north and south, and sit at the table at the kingdom of God, and some who are last will be first, and some who are first will be last."

I think this parable has multiple meanings attached to it. Here Jesus tells people to enter by the narrow door before the door is shut by the master of the house. I think Jesus means here that he is talking about gaining eternal life in heaven. He states that we must enter by the narrow door because the entrance by the narrow door is difficult. I think Jesus tells us here that the way to heaven and eternal life is not easily gained and is only gained by a few. Jesus says that the door is shut and that we are left outside of the gift that is offered to us in the course of our lives if we do not lead our lives as fully developed persons, living righteously and lovingly. For that reason, Jesus says that we will have lost our chance, and the person who is in the house says simply, "I do not know where you come from."

The parable goes on with the persons who want to gain entrance into eternal life in heaven, as responding that they ate and drank with him. This response is clearly inadequate and it reflects the complete intellectual confusion of the persons who want to be with Christ and do not know how. They think that by living their lives eating and drinking in the street is sufficient. Jesus tells them that such a life devoted to self, to self-entertainment and to pleasures will result in a rejection by God, and Jesus says those persons will essentially not only be barred from heaven but thrust out into some sort of condemnation where they will cry and gnash their teeth. They will see Abraham, Isaac, and Jacob and all the prophets of the kingdom of God and they will know they cannot share in eternal joy and happiness. Jesus reminds us at the end that many will come and sit at the table of God, but he very acutely tells us that the first in the estimation of the world could be the last and the last may well be the first in the heavenly kingdom and banquet.

As usual, Jesus reminds us that we cannot judge by appearances and station in life, and tells us that, as usual, that the sinners and tax collectors and prostitutes with whom he was criticized for spending time and socializing could be the first, and that the heads of companies and nations may be the last. Jesus reminds us that the criteria for his judgment sees into the person and does not take account of the exterior. Jesus reminds us that what God sees and fathoms about us and everyone around us is like an x-ray into each of us, from which no one can hide or escape who they really are and what they have done with their lives.

Chapter 33
The Parable of the Choice of Places at the Table

Luke 14: 7–11

Now he told a parable to those who were invited, when he marked how they chose the places of honor, saying to them, "When you are invited by anyone to a marriage feast, do not sit down in a place of honor, lest a more eminent man than you be invited by him; and he who invited you both will come and say to you, 'Give place to this man,' and then you will begin with shame to take the lowest place.

But when you are invited, go and sit in the lowest place, so that when your host comes he may say to you, 'Friend, go up higher." Then you will be honored in the presence of all who sit at table with you. For every one who exalts himself will be humbled, and he who humbles himself will be exalted."

In this parable, Jesus again points to us, how we should lead our lives, and also reminds us of the criteria of how humankind will be judged, and that his standards of judgments are not the world's criteria or the world's standards for judgment. The parable can be summarized as follows. We are told that when we are invited to the marriage feast, we should not sit down in a place of honor, lest a more eminent man at the marriage feast than you be invited by him, and you, at that time, are told to give your place to this man, and you will feel ashamed to take the lowest place. Jesus suggests to us that, when we are invited to the marriage feast we should sit in the lowest place so that when the host comes he will say to you go up higher, and you will then be honored in the presence of all who sit at the table with you. Jesus concludes this parable with the statement that everyone who exalts himself will be humbled and he who humbles himself with exalted.

A number of meanings can be attached to this parable. I think the marriage feast here represents the heavenly banquet, so to speak. In this parable, Jesus tells us that in the kingdom of heaven, and in our lives, we should not raise ourselves above others and that, in fact, if we do that we overestimate ourselves and underestimate others, who may have far greater moral worth than we may know about. The guests who come to this banquet may be a variety of people of various social stations. Jesus suggests to us here that in our lives, if we raise ourselves up in an act of egotism and self-importance, we may well have to give up our station and go to the lowest place, when others we do not know of arrive and are of far greater moral validity as persons, than we are. At that point we will have to give up our place at the table.

This is one sense and interpretation of this parable, that in our lives, and in the kingdom of heaven, we should act with humility, and not raise ourselves above others. Jesus suggests here that in the invitation to this banquet, we should sit in the lowest place, and, when we do so, we will be placed higher and honored in the presence of all at the banquet. The point of the parable is in the final sentence, if in our lives, and when we are in the presence of God, we humble ourselves, we will be exalted, and everyone who exalts themselves will be humbled. Perhaps there are two ways to see this parable and understand it. In one sense, Jesus tells us to be realistic about ourselves and not seek to raise ourselves above others but, in fact, we should humble ourselves in the presence of others. Thus, I think that Jesus suggests that we be realistic with ourselves. A second point in this parable is that when we are humble, God will raise us up, and those who raise themselves up will be humbled. Again Jesus reminds us that God's criterion and judgment on us and others, will not be based on our arrogance, or our egos, or self-importance, or our supposed accomplishments, by which we seek to raise ourselves above others in our own estimation, but he tells us that the judgment will be to exalt the humble and for those who exalt themselves they too will be humbled. Ultimately, Jesus tells us here that in our lives, and in the life to come, we must understand that we are to be humble and that it is the humble that God will reward and raise up, and the proud and arrogant will be brought down and humbled themselves. I think Jesus here is urging us to seek out humility in our lives and understand that God's judgment will be based not on what the world admires, and respects, namely wealth, power and whatever values the world places, but that it is the humble that will be exalted and rewarded.

Perhaps the best way to understand this parable is to understand that Jesus came out of eternity as the ruler of the cosmos and took on the form of a man, with all human limitations attendant upon becoming a person, and that not only did he humble himself to become human, but died an executed criminal to give us eternal life. God's act of humility in becoming a person and dying, not only a natural death, but a tortured and executed death, is a signal to us, as is said in this parable, that it is in humility that we will be raised up as persons.

Chapter 34
The Parable of the Tower Builder and the King Contemplating a Campaign

Luke 14.28–33
"For which of you, desiring to build a tower, does not first sit down and count the cost, whether he has enough to complete it? Otherwise, when he has la id a foundation, and is not able to finish, all who see it begin to mock him, saying, 'This man began to build, and was not able to finish.' Or what king, going to encounter another king in war, will not sit down first and take counsel whether he is able with ten thousand to meet him who comes against him with twenty thousand? And if not, while the other is yet a great way off, he sends an embassy and asks terms of peace. So therefore, whoever of you does not renounce all that he has cannot be my disciple."

In this parable, the connection between the last sentence of advice by Jesus that he who does not renounce all that he has, cannot be my disciple, does not have a clear connection with the previous story picture. In this parable, Jesus says two things: One when you desire to build a tower you should first sit down and count the cost whether you have enough to complete it otherwise when you have laid a foundation and are not able to finish people will make fun of you saying," This man began to build, and was not able to finish." Then in another little story, Jesus says, what king going to encounter another king at war, will not sit down first and take council whether he is able with ten thousand to meet him who comes against him with twenty thousand, and if not, while the other person with twenty thousand is a great way off, he sends an embassy and asks terms of peace.

At first blush, we seem to be told here that we are to act with care and careful preparation. Jesus seems to say here that in general if we go about something we should do so with due consideration that we can accomplish what we wish. In the case with the person who desired to build the tower and did not first sit down and count the cost and is not able to finish people will make fun of him. In the same way, the king who is at war with another king, should be sure that he has the man power to defeat his enemy and, if he do.es not, he must send someone to the embassy and ask for peace.

The last sentence seems to have little connection with these two parables. I think the point being made here is that our lives must be spent in preparation and care of all we do, and ultimately if we do not prepare in our lives for what Jesus may be able to give us in terms of eternal life, and live our lives to the level that he says we are capable of, we will lose out. Of course, this is a general interpretation of these parables and it seems that Jesus says here that in general we should lead our lives and do whatever we do with care and preparation and, on a practical basis, if we do not do so, we will lose out. The last sentence certainly is quite clear that we must give up everything in life or we cannot be a disciple of Christ. What we are asked to renounce certainly includes material goods and whatever things that hold us to ourselves, including our position in society, our families, our spouses, our parents, our intellect, and even our looks should we think those important. The principle enunciated here is that if we wish to follow Christ fully and completely, we must give up everything that stands as a barrier to that.

Chapter 35
The Parable of the Lost Drachma

Luke 15:8–10
"Or what woman, having ten silver coins, if she loses one coin, does not light a lamp and sweep the house and seek diligently until she finds it? And when she has found it, she calls together her friends and neighbors, saying, 'Rejoice with me, for I have found the coin which I had lost.' Just so, I tell you, there is joy before the angels of God over one sinner who repents."

The Parable of the Lost Drachma is one of the finest examples of the message that Jesus seeks out and loves sinners who repent. In this parable, Jesus says that what woman having ten silver coins, if she loses one coin does not light a lamp and sweep the house and seek diligently until she finds it and when she has found it, she calls together her friends and neighbors saying, "Rejoice with me for I have found the coin which I had lost." Jesus ends this parable saying, in the same way, there is joy before the angels of God over one sinner that repents.

In this parable, the woman who lost one silver coin out of ten was probably very poor and losing one coin she looks all over her house for it until she finds it and is so happy that she invites her friends and neighbors where she entertains them. The point of the parable is clear that at the last judgment there will be more joy over one sinner who has repented who had been lost to God. In a sense, Jesus is telling us here that the value that he places on every single human being, regardless of his failings, the depth of his sins, and his degradation in life. The value that God and Christ attaches to every human being is so great that if the person, who was morally lost in his life, on whatever basis he might have failed, nevertheless, there will be great joy, if he repents and therefore is rescued. The joy is so great that God himself surrounded by his angels will together share the great joy that that one person formerly lost has been found.

Chapter 36
The Parable of the Prodigal Son

Luke 15.11–32
And he said, "There was a man who had two sons; and the younger of them said to his father, 'Father, give me the share of property that falls to me.' And he divided his living between them. Not many days later, the younger son gathered all he had and took his journey into a far country, and there he squandered his property in loose living. And when he had spent everything, a great famine arose in that country, and he began to be in want. So he went and joined himself to one of the citizens of that country, who sent him into his fields to feed swine. And he would gladly have fed on the pods that the swine ate and no one gave him anything. But when he came to himself he said, 'How many of my father's hired servants have bread enough and to spare, but I perish here with hunger! I will arise and go to my father, and I will say to him, "Father, I have sinned against heaven and before you; I am no longer worthy to be called your son.' But the father said to his servants, 'Bring quickly the best robe, and put it on him; and put a ring on his hand and shoes on his feet; and bring the fatted calf and kill it, and let us eat and make merry; for this my son was dead, and is alive again; he was lost, and now found.' And they began to make merry.

"Now his elder son was in the field; and as he came and drew near to the house, he heard music and dancing. And he called one of the servants and asked what this meant. And he said to him, 'Your brother has come, and your father has killed the fatted calf because he has received him safe and sound.' But he was angry and refused to go in. His father came out and entreated him, but he answered his father, 'Lo, these many years I have served you, and I never disobeyed your command; yet you never gave me a kid that I might make merry with my friends. But when this son of yours came, who has devoured your living with harlots, you killed for him the fatted calf! And he said to him, Son, you are always with me, and all that is mine is yours. It was fitting to make merry and be glad, for this your brother was dead and is alive; he was lost, and is found."

The Parable of the Prodigal Sons is probably one of the most familiar parables in the Bible to most people. In this parable, Jesus states that there was a man who had two sons, and the younger of the two asked his father, to give him the share of property that was his. The father then divided his living between the two sons and not many days later the younger son gathered all he had and took his journey into a far country where he squandered his property in loose living. When the younger son had spent everything a great famine arouse in that country and he began to be in want and joined himself to one of the citizens of that country who sent him into his fields to feed swine. The younger son would have been happy to feed on the pods that the swine ate and no one gave him anything. When the younger son came to his senses and thought how many of my father's servants have bread enough to spare, but I perish here with hunger. The younger son then said I will rise and go to my father and say I have sinned before heaven and before you. The father, responded to this admission of sin and wrongdoing by his younger son, by saying to his servants to bring the best robe, put it on my son, put a ring on his hand, and shoes on his feet, and bring the fatted calf and kill it, and let us eat and rejoice and make merry for my son who was dead is now alive and he who was lost is now found.

Jesus goes on to say that his elder son was in the field and as he came near to the house he heard music and dancing. He called one of the servants and asked what this meant and the servant explained to him that his brother had come and your father has killed the fatted calf because your father has received him safe and sound. The elder son was angry and refused to go in, even though his father came out and asked him to join the festivities. The elder son said I have served you as my father for many years. I have never disobeyed your command yet you never gave me a feast that I might make merry with my friends. The elder son then states when this son of yours came who had wasted his share of your property living with harlots, you killed for him the fatted cow. The father concludes by saying you are always with me and all that is mine is yours, but it was fitting to rejoice for your brother who was dead is now alive and he who was lost has now been found.

In this parable, there is an earthly father and the younger son asked for his share of his inheritance which came to him, in this case as a gift from his father. Apparently, in this parable, the younger son wanted his full use and possession of his father's property because he wanted to lead his own life. It is not clear whether the younger son is married or not but he seems to be unmarried since no wife is mentioned. Apparently he. dissipates himself in what is called loose living and spends his inheritance completely. It is made clear later in the parable that the loose living mentioned here was spending his time and inheritance with harlots. The younger son is reduced to complete poverty and ends up having to feed swine and cannot even obtain anything to eat and reaches the point where no one will give him anything. He then returns to his father, owns up to his sin and wrongdoing, admits his unworthiness as a son, and the father's response is to immediately forgive his son and give him the best of clothes and shoes and even to give him a feast because this son who was lost and dead is now alive and found.

The returning son is made welcome as a guest and even given a robe, ring and shoes. It is the elder son who is angry that this feast is given for his younger brother and says that he has done everything for his father, has served him, and never disobeyed his commands, and yet his father has never given him a feast like this and the father's response was you are always with me and you can have everything that is mine but this feast for my younger son was given because he was lost to me and dead to me and now returned.

This parable describes once again the grace and unlimited love of God for all men and women. For each of us child, handicapped, old, young, whoever they may be, he sets his unbounded mercy and love for each and every one of us, particularly for the lost sinner who has returned his unlimited love is given even more greatly. As in the Parable of the Lost Drachma, the love of God is even greater when one lost sinner returns. The second part of the parable concerning the response of the older son and his protest, represents the response of men and women who cannot accept the grace and love of God given to another who has offended and has done wrong and who has not lead a righteous life. Jesus tells us in this parable that we cannot protest God's love for the lost. We cannot protest his unbounded mercy and love that extends to the sinner who returns and repents. He commands us here to rejoice and give up our loveless ways and be merciful as God is merciful to the lost sinner. This parable is a paradigm of the gospel which is good news not only for the righteous but more particularly, and greatly for the sinners for whom God's love is even greater and it is them who he seeks out most particularly with the gospel to be saved. God's love is all the greater for the lost who returns and we should not be appalled or jealous at the extent of his love.

Chapter 37
The Parable of the Unjust Steward

Luke 16.1–8
He also said to the disciples, "There was a rich man who had a steward, and charges were brought to him that this man was wasting his goods. And he called him and said to him, 'What is this that I hear about you? Turn in the account of your stewardship, for you can no longer be steward.' And the steward said to himself, 'What shall I do, since my master is taking the stewardship away from me? I am not strong enough to dig, and I am ashamed to beg. I have decided what to do, so that people may receive me into their houses when I am put out of the stewardship.'

So, summoning his master's debtors one by one, he said to the first, 'How much do you owe my master?' He said, 'A hundred measures of oil.' And he said to him, 'Take your bill, and sit down quickly and write fifty.' Then he said to another, 'And how much do you owe?' He said, 'A hundred measures of wheat.' He said to him, 'Take your bill, and write eighty.' The master commended the dishonest steward for his shrewdness; for the sons of this world are more shrewd in dealing with their own generation than the sons of light.

The Parable of the Unjust Steward can be summarized as follows. Jesus says to his disciples that there was a rich man who had a steward and charges were brought to him that this man was wasting his goods. The rich man is then represented as calling the steward and saying to him "What is this I hear about you?" and the rich man then asks him to turn in the account of his stewardship because he can no longer be trusted. The steward then said to himself, "What shall I do, since my master is taking my stewardship away from me?" The steward then says he is not strong enough to dig and is ashamed to beg. The steward then reaches a solution so that people can receive him into their houses.

The steward then summons his master's debtors one by one and says to the first, "How much do you owe my master?" and the debtor answers that he owes a hundred measures of oil and the steward says to the debtor to take his bill, sit down, and write fifty. He then asks another debtor how much he owes and he answers, "A hundred measures of wheat." The steward then says to the debtor to take his bill and write eighty. At the conclusion of the parable, the master commends the dishonest steward for his shrewdness, concluding that the sons of this world are shrewder in dealing with their own generation than the sons of light.

It is not clear what the exact import of this particular parable is. The main point of the parable seems to be the steward to some extent cancelling debts of debtors that owe the master money, or at least, reducing the debts so the steward can obtain entrance into peoples' houses. It is somewhat puzzling that this dishonest steward should be commended for finding a way out of his dishonest actions and its effects? After all, why should this deceitful steward be praised for his escape. Perhaps, it is the mode of escape that is the basis for praise since the steward corrects his deceit by treating his debtors with compassion and thereby reducing the debt. By this method, the steward obtains entrance into peoples' houses and the master commends the dishonest steward for his shrewdness in solving his problem by this act of justice and mercy exhibited to the debtors who apparently owed him money or goods.

The action of the steward was shrewd but also good. The steward essentially committed a crime and solved his problem by acting with consideration to the debtors that owed him debts. The steward acted cleverly and with prudence. The conclusion is that people in the world, perhaps, act better in their dealings with their own group than the sons of light, meaning the righteous or possibly the Christian community. The steward here, in his difficult situation, used his situation to help others.

Perhaps, Jesus is telling us here that what we see as the unrighteous and undesirable, and in this case a criminal, do better with the world system which, in many ways, has a degree of evil attached to it and do better with people who are not necessarily righteous or morally without stain than those in the church with each other. Jesus tells us here that the people in the world can be better people than the church or the religious community. It seems he is also saying that, once again, it may be the sinners who will be saved instead of the righteous or those we think righteous or deserving of salvation. Perhaps, Jesus is telling us that the true church consist of those whose actions are judged good in the end.

Chapter 38
The Parable of the Rich Man and Lazarus

Luke 16.19–31
"There was a rich man, who was clothed in purple and fine linen and who feasted sumptuously every day. And at his gate lay a poor man named Lazarus, full of sores, who desired to be fed with what fell from the rich man's table; moreover the dogs came and licked his sores. The poor man died and was carried by angels to Abraham's bosom. The rich man also died and was buried; and in Hades, being in torment, he lifted up his eyes, and saw Abraham far off and Lazarus in his bosom. And he called out, 'Father Abraham, have mercy upon me, and send Lazarus to dip the end of his finger in water and cool my tongue; for I am in anguish in this flame.' But Abraham said, 'Son, remember that you in your lifetime received your good things, and Lazarus in like manner evil things; but now he is comforted here, and you are in anguish. And besides all this, between us and you a great chasm has been fixed, in order that those who would pass from here to you may not be able, and none may cross from there to us.'

"And he said, 'Then I beg you, father, to send him to my father's house, for I have five brothers, so that he may warn them, lest they also come into this place of torment.' But Abraham said, 'They have Moses and the prophets; let them hear them.' And he said, 'No, Father Abraham; but if someone goes to them from the dead, they will repent.' He said to him, 'If they do not hear Moses and the prophets, neither will they be convinced if someone should rise from the dead.'"

The Parable of the Rich Man and Lazarus is familiar to many people. In this parable, Jesus presents a picture of a rich man in fine clothes who feasted every day in a wonderful way, while at his gate lay a poor man named Lazarus, full of sores, who desired to be fed with what fell from the rich man's table, but only dogs came and licked his sores. The poor man died and was carried by angels to Abraham's bosom. The rich man died as well, and in Hades while in torment, he lifted up his eyes and saw Abraham far off and Lazarus in his bosom. He called out, "Father Abraham, have mercy on me, and send Lazarus to dip the end of his finger in water and cool my tongue," because of the torment he was going through in the flame. Abraham said, "Son, remember that in your life you received good things, and Lazarus received evil things, but now he is comforted here and you are in anguish." Abraham noted that a great barrier had been fixed in order that none of those who had passed from heaven to Hades might cross from heaven to Hades and none might cross from Hades to heaven.

After this, the rich man begged Abraham to send Lazarus to his father's house to warn his brothers about their possibly coming into the place of torment. Abraham replied, "They have Moses and the prophets, let them hear them." The response of the rich man was that if someone rose from the dead his brothers would repent, but Abraham responded that if they do not hear Moses and the prophets, neither would they be convinced if someone rose from the dead.

This parable has a number of meanings that can be gleaned from it. Two will be considered here. One is that if we have the opportunity presented to us in our lives to help and assist those less fortunate than us, we should not waste and spend our lives in our own selfish pleasures as the rich man did in this parable. Jesus also says that if we do this then, we will suffer in the next world.

In the parable, Lazarus is disabled and covered with a skin disease. He is virtually a beggar in the street at the gate of the rich man's house where he desires to be given the leftovers of the feast. Perhaps, what fell from the rich man's table was crumbs or scraps that may have fallen or were thrown from the table for the dogs. The dogs here are licking Lazarus' sores. The initial lesson here is that for ignoring the plight of Lazarus and his miserable condition, the rich man is condemned to some sort of torment in Hades while Lazarus is rewarded in heaven at the bosom of Abraham. In his torment, the rich man begs Abraham to send Lazarus to cool him with his finger in water while in anguish from the flames. Abraham explains that he received good things in his life and Lazarus received evil things so he is now comforted in heaven while the rich man suffers in hell. The implication here is that Lazarus is rewarded with a place in heaven, having suffered greatly during his life, and the rich man is punished. We may conclude that this punishment is for his not showing compassion and love for the suffering and unfortunate. Lazarus was right in front of him in hunger, poverty and physical suffering, while he did nothing to help.

There is a second strand to this parable. This appears when the rich man begs Abraham to send Lazarus to warn his five brothers about what can happen to them and what may be in store for them in torment, Abraham responds that since they have had their chance to hear this message and change their lives through the word of Moses and his prophets, they will not be convinced. Even if someone returns from the dead and warns them it will do them no good and they will remain unconvinced and will not change their lives.

This is an extremely perceptive message that Jesus gives us in the second part of this parable. He says that we all have the chance and opportunity to hear through the Bible and its message who we should be and what we should do with our lives. If, in our lives, we have paid no attention and remained unchanged and unconvinced, Jesus says here, even if someone returns from the dead to tell us about Moses and the prophets and even about Christ, we will remain adamant. Jesus tells us further that we all have a chance to make something of our lives and if we throw away our chance we do so knowingly and intentionally and it is our own fault, and nothing will change who we are and the decisions we have made.

Chapter 39
The Parable of the Servant's Reward

Luke 17: 7-10
"Will anyone of you, who has a servant plowing or keeping sheep, say to him when he has come in from the field, 'Come at once and sit down at table'? Will he not rather say to him, 'Prepare supper for me, and grid yourself and serve me, till I eat and drink; and afterward you shall eat and drink'? Does he thank the servant because he did what was commanded? So you also, when you have done all that is commanded you, say, 'We are unworthy servants; we have only done what was our duty.'"

In this parable known as the Parable of the Servant's Reward, found in Luke 17: 7–10, Jesus asks us who of you who has a servant plowing or keeping sheep will say to him when he comes in from the field, "Come in at once and sit down at the table." Will he not rather say to him, "Prepare supper for me and gird yourself and serve me, until I eat and drink, and afterward you shall eat and drink." The question is asked does he thank the servant because he did what he was commanded. Jesus ends this parable with a statement, "So you also, when you have done all that is commanded of you, say, 'We are unworthy servants; we have only done what was our duty.'"

This parable is somewhat difficult to completely understand. It is somewhat difficult to grasp that the person who has a servant, who is planning on keeping sheep, should not sit down at the table with the servant, which would be the better moral action. The servant's proper role, however, we are told, is to serve the master, prepare his supper, and then the servant can eat and drink. Jesus says here that when the master has a slave or servant who comes in from the fields, it is more likely that the master will command the servant to serve him, and then the servant can eat. Jesus emphasizes that the master will not invite the servant to eat with him. Jesus says that once the servant has done what he is told he does not deserve thanks since that is his duty and role. Jesus concludes that even when we have done what has been commanded of us by God and Christ in our lives, we have only done what we have been told to do and what was our duty.

Jesus concludes here that whatever we do and whatever good works we do, we do out of command and obedience to God, and we remain unworthy and have done nothing to merit God's grace and love. The ultimate lesson here is that God is the one who gives us his love, grace, and compassion and mercy, not because of anything we have done in our lives that has made us in any way worthy, and not because of what we are or have done but because it is God who first loved us. We remain unworthy of his love, which nevertheless is freely and constantly given.

Chapter 40
The Parable of the Unjust Judge

Luke 18. 1–8
And he told them a parable to the effect that they ought always to pray and not lose heart. He said, "In a certain city there was a judge who neither feared God nor regarded man; and there was a widow in that city who kept coming to him and saying, 'Vindicate me against my adversary.' For a while he refused; but afterward he said to himself, 'Though I neither fear God nor regard man, yet because this widow bothers me, I will vindicate her, or she will wear me out by her continual coming.'"

And the Lord said, "Hear what the unrighteous judge says. And will not God vindicate his elect, who cry to him day and night? Will he delay long over them? I tell you, he will vindicate them speedily. Nevertheless, when the Son of Man comes, will he find faith on earth?"

In the Parable of the Unjust Judge, found in Luke 18:1–8, we are told that Jesus told the disciples a parable to the effect that they were always to pray and not lose heart. Jesus said that in a certain city there was a judge who neither feared God nor regarded man and there was a widow in that city who kept coming to him and saying, "Vindicate me against my adversary." For a while the judge refused but afterwards he said to himself, "Though I neither fear God or regard man, yet because this widow bothers me I will vindicate her or she will wear me out by her continual coming." Jesus concludes by saying that God will vindicate his elect who cry to him day and night and will not delay long over them but will vindicate them speedily. Nevertheless, Jesus concludes here and asks the question, "When the Son of Man comes, will he find faith on earth?"

In this parable apparently a widow brought her case to a single judge. What the case was exactly about, we do not know. It may have been, for example, about a debt. She importunes in her impoverished condition the judge to render her justice. The judge finally gives in because of the persistence of the widow in asking him. The lesson here, we are told, is that in the same way, God will hasten to help his elect who cry to him day and night and will save and deliver them.

I think the proper interpretation of this parable is that God wishes us to petition and pray and, if we do so with persistence and faith, he will hear and grant our requests. Jesus advises persistence in our petitions to him and our prayers, and though we cry to him day and night, he will hear our prayers and grant our petitions and will do so speedily without delay.

The last sentence and question here is that, nevertheless, when the Son of Man comes, will he find faith on earth? This has no clear connection with the parable. Still, it is a legitimate question. Will Jesus find faith on earth when he returns to judge the living and the dead? What will be found of humankind at the end of time is an enduring issue. Jesus lays before us that final question. When he returns, will he find faith? That is the question as we look at ourselves, and look at the world around us: what do we really find of faith. Rather, it would appear, as we look around us, we find self-interest, self-involvement, self-love, and outright sin, evil, and degradation. Thus, the question at the end of this parable is very much a pressing and legitimate question and not one to be taken lightly.

Chapter 41
The Parable of the Pharisee and the Publican

Luke 18.9–14
He also told this parable to some who trusted in themselves that they were righteous and despised others: "Two men went up into the temple to pray, one a Pharisee and the other a tax collector. The Pharisee stood and prayed thus with himself, 'God, I thank thee that I am not like other men, extortioners, unjust, adulterers, or even like this tax collector. I fast twice a week, I give tithes of all that I get.' But the tax collector, standing far off, would not even lift up his eyes to heaven, but beat his breast, saying, 'God, be merciful to me a sinner!' I tell you, this man went down to his house justified rather than the other; for everyone who exalts himself will be humbled, but he who humbles himself will be exalted."

In the Parable of the Pharisee and the Publican, the parable was addressed to some who trusted in themselves that they were righteous and despised others. In the parable, we are told that two men went up in the temple to pray, one a Pharisee and the other a tax collector. We are told the Pharisee stood and prayed by himself saying, "God, I thank thee that I am not like other men: extortioners, unjust, adulterers, or even like this tax collector." The Pharisee said, "I fast twice a week, and give tithes of all that I get." The tax collector standing far off would not even lift his eyes to heaven, but beat his breast saying, "God, be merciful to me a sinner." Jesus tells us that the tax collector went down to his house justified, rather than the other, and concludes that everyone who exalts himself will be humbled but he who humbles himself will be exalted.

The point of the parable is fairly clear. The Pharisee incorrectly raises himself above the common mass and points out how he gives money away and even fasts. So to speak, the Pharisee beats his chest about himself and his good deeds in comparison to the people around him whose failings he points out. The Pharisee points out his self-denial. Then we are told the tax collector seeks mercy from God as a sinner.

The point here is quite clear. God does not want self-love or self-adulation, does not want us to raise ourselves above others with false pride, and certainly does not want us to have pride and the sense of importance and superiority that the Pharisee exhibits. Instead, Jesus recommends that we be humble and realize our sinful condition. He ends with the lesson and advice that the humble will be exalted and, like the Pharisee, everyone who exalts himself will be humbled.

Clearly, God wants from us sincerity, not pride, and a realization of our human limitations and failings, rather than a vision of ourselves as better than the others who surround us. Jesus tells us that it is in humility that we will know God, and that the self-righteous and proud will in the end be brought down. Jesus teaches us here that it is not by our supposed good deeds, in comparison to the failings and defects of others, but by the realization of our failed human condition that we will be raised up from our humble station and that the proud and powerful, who thought themselves in control and beyond others, will be humbled.

Appendix I
The Ten Commandments or The Decalogue

Exodus 20.1–17

And God spoke all these words, saying, "I am the Lord your God, who brought you out of the land of Egypt, out of the house of bondage.

"You shall have no other gods before me."

"You shall not make for yourself a graven image, or any likeness of anything that is in heaven above, or that is in the earth beneath, or that is in the water under the earth; you shall not bow down to them or serve them; for I the Lord your God am a jealous God, visiting the iniquity of the fathers upon the children to the third and the fourth generation of those who hate me, but showing steadfast love to thousands of those who love me and keep my commandments.

"You shall not take the name of the Lord your God in vain; for the Lord will not hold him guiltless who takes his name in vain."

"Remember the Sabbath day, to keep it holy. Six days you shall labor, and do all your work; but the seventh day is a Sabbath to the Lord your God; in it you shall not do any work, you, or your son, or your daughter, your manservant, or your maidservant, or your cattle, or the sojourner who is within your gates; for in six days the Lord made heaven and earth, the sea, and all that is in them, and rested the seventh day; therefore the Lord blessed the Sabbath day and hallowed it.

"Honor your father and your mother, that your days may be long in the land which the Lord your God gives you.

"You shall not kill.

"You shall not commit adultery.

"You shall not steal.

"You shall not bear false witness against your neighbor.

"You shall not covet your neighbor's house; you shall not covet your neighbor's wife, or his manservant, or his maidservant, or his ox, or his ass, or anything that is your neighbor's."

The Ten Commandments, or the Decalogue, represent extremely advanced ethical and moral thinking. The First Commandment forbids the worship of any other gods other than the Jewish God, Jehovah or Yaweh. It is clear that this commandment involves, suggests, and virtually commands monotheism, since other gods are out of the question. There is only one God who has created everything, and who is the source of all justice and power. This commandment sets apart the Hebrew nation and their concept of God and is in opposition to any sort of polytheism.

The Second Commandment forbids the making and worship of a graven image, or more exactly a carved image of wood or stone. The Jewish God is a spiritual being and cannot be represented by anything material. Like the First Commandment, which is monotheistic in its command, the Second Commandment is equally advanced in its concept of God as a spirit. The nations surrounding the Jewish nation embraced idolatry on a grand scale, and as I said, were largely polytheistic in their orientation. This commandment again focuses on the Jewish nation's difference.

The Third Commandment prohibits any misuse of God's name in perjury, or making vows and not keeping them. Again, this commandment is extremely, intellectually, and spiritually advanced, since it is directed to intellectual and spoken word misuse.

The Fourth Commandment enjoins the keeping of the seventh day as a holy day of sacrifice and festival.

The Fifth Commandment speaks of the respect and obligation due to parents by their children. This commandment is not only addressed to young children honoring their parents but to those of any age who have parents. In particular, this commandment concerns children's caring for and respecting old and weak parents. Again, this is an extremely advanced ethic. The use of the word *honor* is particularly compelling and involves a deep-seated intellectual, if not spiritual, obligation on the part of children to their parents.

The Sixth Commandment refers to murder but not to killing, war, or capital punishment. See Deuteronomy, Chapter 20.1ff and Exodus 21.1ff.

The Seventh Commandment refers to adultery within marriage, with another man's wife. See Leviticus 18.20, 20.10 and Deuteronomy 22.22.

The Eighth Commandment prohibits stealing and is quite clear.

The Ninth Commandment apparently prohibits perjury in the law courts but might be interpreted as a reference to simply injuring a person's good name by making false statements about him. See Deuteronomy 19.16–21. Once again this commandment, speaking falsely in general about someone else with the intent to injure their reputation, represents an extreme advance in ethical and moral thinking.

The Tenth Commandment is most a significant moral advance in thinking since it attacks a thought pattern of envy, which is a weakness that all men and women share. The commandment seems to concern itself with our innermost thoughts and desires.

The Decalogue is unique in the advanced thinking it represents. In its time it was unique and remains so to this day. Jesus, many times, extended the Decalogue, in his interpretation of it. For example, in Matthew 5.21–23, Jesus says that the commandment not to kill is extended to the point that everyone who is angry with his brother shall be liable to judgment; whoever insults his brother shall be liable to council; and whoever says, "You fool," shall be liable to the hell fire. Jesus says, in Matthew 5.27 in extension of the commandment not to commit adultery, that everyone who looks at a woman lustfully has already committed adultery with her in his heart. Further, in Matthew 5.31–32, Jesus states that everyone who divorces his wife, except on grounds of unchastity, makes her an adulteress and whoever marries a divorced woman commits adultery. These statements of Jesus are in relation to the older rule stated in verse 31, that whoever divorces his wife should give her a certificate of divorce. Jesus says, in Matthew 5.33, with respect to the statement not to swear falsely, not to swear at all but simply to say yes or no. In Matthew 5.38, Jesus' comment on the rule eye for an eye and tooth for a tooth, says that we should not resist evil, but if someone strikes us on the right cheek we should turn to him the other. Finally, in Matthew 5.43–44, Jesus says of the rule that we should love our neighbor and hate our enemies, rather that we should love our enemies and pray for those who persecute us. See also on Jesus' extension of the Decalogue, Matthew 18.21; Matthew 19.16–22; Mark 7.14, Mark 9.42–48; Mark 10.1–9.

What I have analyzed here and spoken about represent my thoughts, first, on the extremely advanced thinking reflected in the Decalogue. Second, I also comment on Jesus' extremely advanced extension of these moral rules to the point, in many ways, of making the fulfillment of them almost impossible. It is hoped that this discussion of the Decalogue, its interpretation and Jesus' extension of it, is related in turn to the extremely advanced commandments and thinking reflected in the parables. In short, in the parables we have Jesus' advanced thinking beyond the Decalogue, which is also reflected in these sections of the gospels that I have discussed here, which set forth Jesus' interpretation and extension of the Decalogue.

Appendix II
The Sermon on the Mount

Matthew 5.1-11

Seeing the crowds, he went up on the mountain, and when he sat down his disciples came to him. And he opened his mouth and taught them, saying:

"Blessed are the poor in the spirit, for theirs is the kingdom of heaven.

"Blessed are those who mourn, for they shall be comforted.

"Blessed are the meek, for they shall inherit the earth.

"Blessed are those who hunger and thirst for righteousness, for they shall be satisfied.

"Blessed are the merciful, for they shall obtain mercy.

"Blessed are the pure in heart, for they shall see God.

"Blessed are the peacemakers, for they shall be called sons of God.

"Blessed are those who are persecuted for righteousness' sake, for theirs is the kingdom of heaven.

"Blessed are you when men revile you and persecute you and utter all kinds of evil against you falsely on my account."

Luke 6.20-22

And he lifted up his eyes on his disciples, and said:

"Blessed are you poor, for yours is the kingdom of God.

"Blessed are you that hunger now, for you shall be satisfied.

"Blessed are you that weep now, for you shall laugh.

"Blessed are you when men hate you, and when they exclude you and revile you, and cast out your name as evil, on account of the Son of Man!"

I have included the two versions of the Sermon on the Mount, found in Matthew 5.1–11 and Luke 6.20–22. I have included the Sermon on the Mount here because it is clearly connected to the advanced moral and ethical thinking I have discussed in the parables.

The Sermon on the Mount partakes of poetry. The version in Matthew is longer than the version in Luke. The beatitudes are not a set of moral rules, but a speech directing us to the right life and the promises of the kingdom for those who follow the beatitudes. The beatitudes all involve the use of the word "blessed" or "blessing." In Matthew 5.3, Jesus says the poor in spirit are blessed and theirs will be the kingdom of heaven. Poor in spirit probably refers to humility or weakness, if not poverty. Matthew 5.4 states that those who mourn shall be comforted and are blessed; this probably refers to anyone who is oppressed and as a result is in mourning. In Matthew 5.5, the meek are pronounced blessed and it is stated that they will inherit the earth. Again this seems to refer to the humble inheriting the earth, meaning entering into the new kingdom to be established by Christ.

The rest of the beatitudes in Matthew 5 are clear and radical in their orientation. In verse 6, we are told that those who hunger and thirst for righteousness in this world shall be satisfied in the next, and that those who are merciful in this life shall obtain mercy in the next. In verse 8, again we are told that the pure in heart are blessed and shall see God and, in verse 9, that the peacemakers are blessed and shall be called Sons of God. In verse 10, we are told that those who are persecuted for righteousness' sake shall be in the kingdom of God.

As a comment on the Sermon on the Mount and on the beatitudes, most of the beatitudes seem to involve some sort of reciprocity. Jesus says in Matthew 5 that the humble and those who seek after righteousness in this life and those who are merciful in this life, those who are pure in heart, and those who are peacemakers, and those who are persecuted for their righteousness, shall be rewarded, and as it were, rule and be fulfilled in the next world.

The beatitudes in Luke 6.20–22 are shorter. I have this to say in particular: in Luke 6.20, Jesus does not say that the poor in spirit are blessed and will have the kingdom of heaven but that the poor will be blessed and have the kingdom of heaven. The remainder of the beatitudes in Luke follow to some extent the format in Matthew but are slightly different, but are equally reciprocal. Thus there is the statement in Luke 6.21 that if you hunger now you will be satisfied in the next world, and if you weep now you shall laugh in the next. Jesus seems to say here that those in poverty and that those who suffer in this life will rejoice, be satisfied, and literally have the kingdom of God in the next. Jesus seems to say in Luke 6.20–22, that those in this life who may seem to be of no worth and value, and who suffer the most, will be rewarded in the next life above all others. Finally, in verse 22, Jesus states that you are blessed when men hate you and when they exclude you and revile you and cast out your name as evil on account of the Son of Man. This last verse tells us that when Christians are persecuted in this world and in this life they will be blessed in the next and even rewarded for their suffering.

The summary here of the main thoughts, thrusts, and teachings by Jesus in the Sermon on the Mount reveals an extremely advanced moral vision and an extremely advanced thought in general. Jesus' teachings in the Sermon on the Mount paint a world and reveal a system of thought far beyond, perhaps, any contemporary thinking at that time or at any time. Jesus' statements in the Sermon on the Mount that humility and poverty are somehow blessed and that those in poverty and in humility will inherit the kingdom of heaven will always challenge and disturb the world and its valuation system. There are many teachings in the Sermon on the Mount, but this much can be said, that the vision of life presented by Jesus in the Sermon on the Mount represents a radical, if not revolutionary, break from most forms of thinking.

Appendix III
Additional Reflections

After I completed the book on the Parables of Jesus, it came to my mind that I wish to speak about some other topics. It is my thought that these topics will be of significant interest to the general public, to the church at large, and to the Christian community. What I propose to speak about are two things.

One: The status of women as it is presented in both the Hebrew Bible and the New Testament. Although I have concluded that many people take certain statements of Saint Paul as anti-woman, a closer examination of both the Hebrew Bible and the New Testament, particularly what is recorded about Jesus and his many relationships with many women, reveals a totally different picture, and perhaps a more accurate one.

Second, I would like to speak about sexuality and marriage in Christian thought. For believing Christians in general, it is marriage or a single life without sex. I propose to give an explanation of this, since this particular teaching is rather hard since all of us have sexual feelings about the opposite sex. What I propose to explain and point out here is that sexuality (and frankly there is nothing wrong with sex) for a Christian is channeled into love and the family. The present emphasis in the modern world on rampant sexuality leads nowhere. I think that it is the intention of God to use sexual feelings and direct them to love and the family, perhaps in the same way he uses greed and avarice to build society and create jobs for people. I will go further into this in the essay that I propose to present.

The Status of Women

Many people in our present society make the claim that the church is anti-woman. This statement is largely based on the position of the Roman Catholic

Church and several other churches such as the Orthodox Church and certain more conservative Protestant denominations that do not ordain women to the priesthood or ministry. More to the point, many people have lighted upon certain statements or comments of Saint Paul about women in his letters. For example, in his first letter to the Corinthian Church, in Chapter 7:39, Saint Paul states that a wife is bound to her husband as long as he lives, but that if her husband dies, she is free to marry whomever she wishes. In that same letter in Chapter 11:3-15, Saint Paul states that the head of a woman is her husband. He further states that any woman who prays or prophesies with her head unveiled is dishonoring her head, and that if a woman will not veil herself, then she should cut off her hair. Saint Paul further states that woman is the glory of man and that woman was created for man. He then concludes that that is why a woman ought to have a veil on her head and that in the Lord a woman is not independent of man.

Saint Paul further states in the letter to Ephesians 5:22 that wives should be subject to their husbands because the husband is the head of the wife, and wives should be subject in everything to their husbands. He further states that husbands should love their wives. In the first letter to the Corinthians 14:34, Saint Paul states that women should keep silence in the churches, since they are not permitted to speak, but should be subordinate, and that it is shameful for a woman to speak in the church. In the letter to the Colossian church Chapter 3:18, Saint Paul again states that wives should be subject to their husbands.

These statements of Saint Paul must be weighed against the entire revelation of the Bible about women and their completely equal status. In Genesis 2 we are told that a woman is created as a helper for a man. This statement does not mean inequality. It simply means that women in the world have a slightly different role than men. Women create homes and raise families. This does not mean that this activity is inferior or less important than other activities.

The book of Judges 4: 5 tells the story of the Judge Deborah, who, as a wife, was judging Israel. It is quite clear that this particular story and the event should be read, not as relegating a woman to a lesser status, since in fact Deborah had a high societal role in Israel.

Let us now look at Jesus' relationships with women in the Gospels. In Matthew 2 we are told about the birth of Jesus to Mary. The fact that God himself chose to be born of a woman is a statement of the real status of woman in the eyes of God, since the very son of God was born of a woman and had a mother.

In Matthew 5:27, Jesus again raises the status of woman in saying that everyone who looks at a woman lustfully has already committed adultery with her. Again, in verse 31 Jesus states that anyone who divorces his wife, except on the ground of un-chastity, makes her an adulteress, and whoever marries a divorced woman commits adultery. Once again, Jesus Christ is significantly raising the status of women in the world.

In Matthew 15:21, Jesus heals the daughter of a societal outcast a Canaanite woman. In Matthew 27:55, Matthew says that many women follow

Jesus from Galilee, among whom were Mary Magdalene and Mary, the mother of James and Joseph. In chapter 28, Mary Magdalene and Mary went to see the Sepulchral after the crucifixion.

In Mark 15:40, we are told that many women looked on Jesus on the cross from afar, including Mary Magdalene and Mary. Earlier when he was in Galilee, they followed him and ministered to him, and many other women came up with him to Jerusalem. Again in Mark 16, we are told that Mary Magdalene and Mary were at the tomb of Christ after his crucifixion.

In Luke 1, we are told of the birth of Christ. See also Luke 2:15. In Luke 7:37 we are given the story that a woman of the city, who is a sinner, brings a flask of ointment and, standing at Jesus' feet, wets his feet with her tears, wipes them with the hair of her head, and kisses his feet and anoints them in the ointment. The Pharisees say, "What sort of person are you? Associating with this sinner?" and Jesus points out to Simon that when he had entered Simon's house, he had been given no water for his feet, but this woman has wet his feet with her tears and wiped them with her hair. Jesus says, "You gave me no kiss, but from the time I came, she has not ceased to kiss my feet. And you did not anoint my head with oil, but she has anointed my feet with ointment." In Luke 10:38–42, we are told that Martha received Jesus into her house and that she had sister called Mary who sat at Jesus' feet and listened to his teaching. In Luke 23:36, we are told that the women who followed Jesus from Galilee stood before him from a distance at the crucifixion.

In John 8, we are told of a story of a woman caught in adultery, and of Jesus' preventing her execution. In John 12 again we are told the story of Martha and Mary, that six days before the Passover Jesus came to Bethany and that Martha served Jesus and Mary anointed the feet of Jesus with ointment and wiped his feet with her hair. See also John 19:25 and John 21.

This essay, although it is basic and superficial in its examination of the status of women in the church, reveals, I think, quite clearly that in both the Hebrew bible and the Gospels women have an equal status in society. Jesus apparently had many woman friends and women who followed him and with whom he had relationships. The passages that I have taken from the gospels clearly reveal that, to put it bluntly, Jesus had no problem with women.

Thus, what I have just taken from the Gospels and the Hebrew Bible, should be weighed against the statements of Saint Paul. Saint Paul was addressing particular situations in the churches he had established. Perhaps his comments about the role of woman may have emanated from his background and culture, which had a slightly different view of the role of women in society.

My conclusion is that Jesus not only had woman friends but, significantly, by his actions raised the status of woman in his culture.

Sexuality and Marriage in the Christian Culture

In our present culture, sex is a hot topic. The reason for this is that sex has become associated with commerce or money or, better put, sex sells! Every magazine in a store we see has a picture of a rather sexually attractive woman. Often the movies that are produced seem to feature young, sexually attractive women and men. Our society in the media rarely features elderly people. So, one might say that sex is a topic and image that is not merely prevalent in our culture, but literally we are inundated with sexual images almost every day in American society. I have no argument with this myself, but I merely make this observation.

There are some people who, barraged with these images and pounded with this sexual message, may come to think that free sexual promiscuity is the thing to do and way to live. Obviously, this might be a mistake, although I make no moral judgment on the person who wishes to shape their lives in this way, since we live in a free society, and unless the action is illegal, it is permitted. I do add that most people have the wish to and do get married at some point in their lives. What I propose to discuss here is sex and marriage for a Christian and in the church.

My view is that sexual attraction and, or even lust, is something that we cannot deal with without direction and control. To be hungry and to wish to eat is fine, but no one would recommend that we eat all the time to the point of gorging ourselves. The same is true of sexual activity or sexual desire. It is not something that we can simply do with anyone or at any time we want.

For the Christian, God directs lust and sexual desire to a loving union with the opposite sex and to the creation of the family. In the same way that we cannot eat anywhere, at any time we want, for the Christian, God channels lust and desire to a loving relationship and a union which ultimately evolves into the creation of a family.

I said in the introduction that God uses avarice and greed to create jobs and employment. In spending money and in making money for ourselves, there is a benefit to others in the community through job creation and job maintenance. One may conclude that God uses what can be misused and brings people together in love. Sex unlimited goes nowhere and leads to a kind of destruction. Sex directed in love and in the family union, properly channeled, is God's plan and it is the only possible alternative to societal chaos.

Select Bibliography

Abrahams, Israel. *Studies in Pharisaism and the Gospels.* Cambridge, UK: Cambridge University Press, 1917.
Albertz, Martin. *Die synoptischen Streitgesprache.* Berlin: Nabu, 1921.
Bailey, Kenneth E. *Through Peasant Eyes: More Lucan Parables, Their Culture and Style.* Grand Rapids: Eerdmans, 1980.
Barclay, William. *The Parables of Jesus.* Westminster: John Knox Press, 1999.
Beare, Francis Wright. *Earliest Record of Jesus.* N.p.: Abingdon, 1962.
Bloomberg, Craig L. *Interpreting the Parables.* Downers Grove: InterVarsity, 1990.
Brouwer, A. M. *De Gelijkenissen.* Leiden, 1946.
Browne, L. E. *The Parables of the Gospels in the Light of Modern Criticism.* Cambridge, UK: Cambridge University Press, 1913.
Bruce, Alexander. B. *The Parabolic Teaching of Jesus Christ.* New York: A.C. Armstrong and Son, 1882.
Bugge, Christian. A. *Die Haupt-Parabeln Jesu.* Geissen, 1903.
Bultmann, Rudolf. *Die Geschichte der Synoptischen Tradition.* Gottingen, 1931. Translated by John Marsh, UK: S.C.M., 1963.
Cadoux, Arthur T. *The Parables of Jesus.* 1930.
Crossan, John Dominic. *In Parables: The Challenge of the Historical Jesus.* New York: Harper & Row, 1973.
Dads, M. *The Parables of Our Lord.* Vol. 1, 1833. Vol. 2, 1909.
Danby, Herbert. *The Mishnah: Translated from the Hebrew with Introduction and Brief Explanatory Notes.* London: Oxford, 1933.
Dibelius, M. *From Tradition to Gospel.* London: Ivor Nicholson & Watson, 1934.
Dodd, C.H. *The Parables of the Kingdom.* New York: Charles E. Scribner, 1935.
Drummond, James. *The Parables of Jesus.* 1917.
Drury, John. *The Parables in the Gospels: History and Allegory.* New York: Crossroad, 1985.
Easton, B.S. *The Gospel before the Gospels.* New York: Charles E. Scribner, 1929.
Fiebig, P. *Altjudische Gleichnisse und die Gleichnisse Jesu.* Tubingen: Mohr, 1904.
———. *Der Erzahlungsstil der Evangelien.* Leipzig: Mohr, 1925.

———. *Die Gleichnisreden Jesu im Lichte der Rabbinischen Gleichnisse des Neutestamentlichen Zeitalters.* Leipzig: Mohr, 1912.
———. *Rabbinische Gleichnisse.* Leipzig: Mohr, 1929.
Feldman, Asher. *The Parables and Similes of the Rabbis.* Cambridge: University Press, 1927.
Findlay, J. A. *Jesu and His Parables.* London: Epworth, 1950.
Funk, Robert W. *Parables and Presence.* Philadelphia: Fortress, 1982.
Goebel, S. *Die Parabeln Jesu.* Almanach de Gotha, 1879. English Translation, 1883.
Gresswell, Edward. *An Exposition of the Parables and of Other Parts of the Gospels.* 6 vols. Oxford: Rivington, 1834–35.
Gundry, Robert H. *Matthew: A Commentary on His Handbook for a Mixed Church under Persecution.* Grand Rapids: Eerdmans, 1994.
Hagner, Donald A. *Matthew.* 2 vols. Dallas: Word, 1993, 1995.
Hauck, F. In Kittel's *Theologisches Worterbuch zum Neuen Testament,* by Gerhard Kittel. 5:741f. Kohlhammer, 1990.
Hoskyns, E., and F. N. Davey. *The Riddle of the New Testament.* London: Faber, 1931.
Hunter, Archibald M. *Interpreting the Parables.* London: SCM, 1960.
———. *The Work and Words of Jesus.* London: SCM, 1950.
Jeremias, Joachim. *Die Gleichnisse Jesu.* Zurich: Zwingli Verlag, 1954.
———. *The Parables of Jesus.* Translated by S. H. Hooke. (Published in several revised editions.) Second revised edition, New York: Scribner's, 1954.
Jones, Ivor H. *The Matthean Parables: A Literary and Historical Commentary.* (NovTSup 80). Leiden: Brill, 1995.
Jülicher, Adolf. *Die Gleichnisreden Jesu.* 2 vols. Tubingen: Mohr, 1899.
Kissinger, Warren S. *The Parables of Jesus: A History of Interpretation and Bibliography.* Metuchen, NJ: Scarecrow, 1979.
Kümmel, Werner G. *Promise and Fulfilment.* Translated by D.M. Burton. London: SCM, 1957.
Manson, T. W. *The Sayings of Jesus.* London: SCM, 1949.
Martin, Hugh. *Parables of the Gospel and Their Meaning for Today.* New York: Abingdon, 1937.
McArthur, Harvey K., and Robert M. Johnston. *They Also Taught in Parables: Rabbinic Parables from the First Centuries of the Christian Era.* Grand Rapids: Zondervan, 1990.
McFadyen, J. M. *The Parables* (Bruce Lectures). 1932.
Montefiore, Claude G. *Rabbinic Literature and Gospel Teaching.* London: Macmillan, 1930.
———. *The Synoptic Gospels.* London: Macmillan, 1909.
Moulton, Warren J. In *Dictionary of Christ and the Gospels.* Edited by James Hastings, 1930. Reprinted Honolulu, University Press of the Pacific, 2:312 f, 2004.
New Testament Studies
Oesterley, William. O. E. *The Synoptic Parables in the Light of Their Jewish Background.* London: Society for Promoting Christian Knowledge, 1936.
"Parables of the Gospels: Artist, Eugene Burnand (1850–1921)." *St. Joseph Magazine* 58 (1957): 23–30.
"The Parables of the New Testament." *Dublin Review* 27 (1849):181–227.
Parables, Told by Our Lord, Arranged by Nan Dearmer. London: Faber & Faber, 1944.
The Parables Told to the People by Jesus of Nazareth as Recorded in the Gospels. New York: Harper, 1942.
Les Paraboles: Commentaries de M. Philibert. Paris: Editions Siloe, 1952.

Les Paraboles de Jesus. Canada: Apostolat de la presse, n.d.
Les Paraboles de l'attente et de la misericorde. Paris: Ligue Cath. de l'Evangile, 1968.
Les Paraboles du Christ: fetes et saisons (Sept-Oct. 1957).
Paramo, S. del. "El fin de las parabolas de Cristo y el Salmo 17." *Comillas* 2 (1967): 95–123. Also, *Miscelanea Comillas* 20 (1953): 233–56.
Parker, S. A. "Thoughts on the Parables; Sermon." *Homiletic and Pastoral Review* 52 (1951): 51–54.
Parroy, Henry. *Recits evangeliques: Les Paraboles.* Paris: Vitte, 1954.
Patten, Priscilla C. "Parable and Secret in the Gospel of Mark in Light of Select Apocalyptic Literature." PhD diss., Drew University, 1976.
Paulli, Jakob. *Jesu Liknelser. En Uppbyggelsebok. Bemynd. Ofvers af Abraham Ahlen.* Stockholm: A. V. Carlson, 1911.
Pedersen, S. "Er Mark 4 et Lignelsekapitel?" *Dansk Teologisk Tiddsskrift* 33 (1970): 20–30.
――――. "Lignelse Eller allegori: Eksegetiskhomiletiske Overvejelser." *Svensk Teologisk Kvartalskrift* 48 (1972): 63–68.
――――. "Den Nytestamentlige Ligneelsesforsknings Metodeproblemer." *Dansk Teologisk Tidsskrift* 28 (1965): 146–84.
Peisker, C. H. "Konsekutives Iva in Markus 4, 12." *Zeitschrift fur die neutestamentliche Wissenschaft* 59 (1968): 126-27.
Percy, Ernst. "Liknelseteorien in Mark 4, 11f. Och Kompositionen av Mark 4, 1–34." In Johannes Lindblom, *Lund. pa hans 65-arsdag den 7 iuni 1947 (Svensk exegetisk arsbok,* XII, 1947):, 242–62; Uppsala: Wretmans boktryckeri A. -B., 1948. Also, *Svensk Exegetisk Asrbok* 12 (1947): 258–78.
Perella, G. M. "Le parabole in particolare." *Palestra del Clerc* 20, 1(1941): 265–69; 20, 2 (1941): 137–46, 281–88; 21, 1(1942): 97–98, 129–32, 193–96, 241–46; 21,2 (1942): 33–40, 97–102, 113–17, 223–27; 22, 1(1943): 49–52, 65–67, 180–83; 22, 2 (1943): 49–54, 145–50, 209–15, 225–29.
Perkins, Pheme. "Interpreting Parables: The Bible and the Humanities." In *Emerging Issues in Religious Education,* edited by Gloria Durka and Jeanmarie Smith, 149–72. New York: Paulist, 1976.
Perrin, Norman. "Biblical Scholarship in a New Vein: Review of Dan O. Via., Jr., *The Parables: Their Literary and Existential Dimension."* *Interpretation* 21 (1967):465–69.
――――. "The Evangelist's Interpretation of Jesus' Parables." *Journal of Religion* 52 (1972): 361–75. Also, *Theology Digest* 21(1973): 146–49.
――――. "Historical Criticism, Literary Criticism, and Hermeneutics; The Interpretation of the Parables of Jesus and the Gospel of Mark Today." *Journal of Religion* 52 (1972): 361–75.
――――. *Jesus and the Language of the Kingdom: Symbol and Metaphor* in *New Testament Interpretation.* Philadelphia: Fortress Press, 1976.
――――. "The Modern Interpretation of the Parables of Jesus and the Problem of Hermeneutics." *Interpretation* 25 (1971): 131–48.
Peruzzi, Angelo. *Studio delle sette parabole in S. Matteo c. 13, owero ii regno dei cieli in esse rivealto e sue fasi.* Torre Pellice: Tip. Alpina, 1924.
Petersen, Norman R. "On the Notion of Genre in Via's Parable and Example Story: A Literary-Structuralist Approach" *Semeia* 1(1974): 134–81.
Petuchowski, J. J. "La signification theologique de la parabole dans la literature rabbinique et dans le NT." *Nouvelles Chretiennes d'Israel* 23 (1972): 76–87.
――――. "The Theological Significance of the Parable in Rabbinic Literature and the

New Testament." *Christian News from Israel* 23 (1972): 76–86.
Pewtress, Vera. *Jesu Liknelser. Overs. av Borje Forsberg och Karl-Erik Brattgard.* Stockholm: Diakonistyr, 1961.
Pfaff, C. M. *Commentatio de recta Theologiae parabolicae et allegoricae conformatione.* Tubingen: 1720.
Pfendsack, Werner. *Ihr aber seid Bruder. Gleichnisse des Lukas-Evangelium.* Basel: F. Reinhardt, 1962.
———. *Die Kirche bleibt nicht im Dorf. Gleichnisse des Matthaus-Evangeliums, ausgelegt fur die Gemeinde.* Basel: F. Reinhardt, 1968.
Pieper, F. "Die Schatzkammer der Gleichnisse Christi." *Chrysologus* 32 (1938–39): 137–39.
Pierson, H. *Geliikenissen des Heeren's Hage: W. A. Beschoor.* Amsterdam: W. ten Have, 1919.
Piper, Otto A. "The Understanding of the Synoptic Parables." *Evangelical Quarterly* 14 (1942): 42–53.
Pirot, Jean. *Allegories et paraboles dans le vie et l'ensignement de Jesus-Christ.* Marseille: Imprimerie Marseillaise, 1943.
———. *Paraboles et allegories evangeliques. Le pensee de Jesus. Les commentaires patristiques.* Paris: Lethielleux, 1949.
Plummer, A. "Parable." In *A Dictionary of the Bible*, edited by James Hastings, 3: 662–65. New York: Scribner's, 1900.
Poovey, William A. *Mustard Seeds and Wine Skins: Dramas and Meditations on Seven Parables.* Minneapolis: Augsburg, 1972.
Poteat, Edwin M. *Parables of Crisis.* New York: Harper, 1950.
Poynder, Augustus. "Mark IV, 12." *Expository Times* 15(1903–04): 141–42.
Prager, M. "Israel in the Parables." *Bridge* 4 (1962): 44–88.
Prins, J. L. "Matth. XIII, 10b: 'Waarom spreekt gij tot hen in gelijkenissen?'" *Theologisch tijdschrift* 18 (1884): 25–38.
Procter, W. C. *Scriptural Similes Classified and Considered.* London: Stanley Martin, 1930.
Provero, Mario. *Le Parabole evangeliche ed ii lore messaggio.* Jerusalem: Franciscan Printing, 1974.
Pryor, J. W. "Markan Parable Theology: An Inquiry into Mark's Principles of Redaction." *Expository Times* 83 (1972): 242–45.
Quick, Oliver C. *The Realism of Christ's Parables: Ida Hartley Lectures Delivered at Colne, Lanes, October 1930.* London: Student Christian Movement Press, 1937.
Schmidt, Karl L. *Der Rahmen der Geschichte Jesu*, 1919. Reprint, Wissenschaftliche Buchgesellscha, 1964.
Schutz, Roland. *Der Parallele Bau der Satzglieder im Neuen Testament.* Gottingen: Vandenhoeck & Ruprecht, 1920.
Sider, John W. *Interpreting the Parables: A Hermeneutical Guide to Their Meaning.* Grand Rapids: Zondervan, 1990.
Smith, B. T. D. *The Parables of the Synoptic Gospels.* University Press: 1937.
Spurgeon, C. H., and Charles Cook, eds. *New Library of Sermons on the Parables.* Grand Rapids: Zondervan: 1958.
Strack, W., and P. Billerbeck. *Kommentar zum Neuen Testament aus Talmud und Midrasch.* Tubingen, 1922.
Swete, Henry B. *Parables of the Kingdom.* New York: Macmillan, 1920.
Taylor, Vincent. *The Formation of the Gospel Tradition.* New York: Macmillan, 1933.
van Koetsveld, C. E. *De Gelijkenissen van den Zaligmaker.* Schoonhoven, 1869.

Via, Dan O. Jr. *The Parables: Their Literary and Existential Dimension.* Philadelphia: Fortress, 1967.
Zeitschrift fur Neutestamentliche Wissenschaft

Index of Biblical Citations

Colossians 3.18, **116**
I Corinthians 7.39, **116**
I Corinthians 11.3–15, **116**
I Corinthians 14.34, **116**

Ephesians 5.22, **116**
Exodus 20.1–17, **107**

Genesis 2, **116**

John 8, **117**
John 12, **117**
John 19.25, **117**
John 21, **117**
Judges 4.5, **116**

Luke 1, **117**
Luke 2.15, **117**
Luke 6.20–22, **111**
Luke 6.47–49, **23**
Luke 7.31–35, **25**
Luke 7.36–48, **71**
Luke 7.37, **117**
Luke 8.4–15, **1**
Luke 10.25-37, **75**
Luke 10.38–42, **117**
Luke 11.5-8, **77**
Luke 11.24–26, **27**
Luke 12. 16-21, **79**

Luke 12.35–40, **17**
Luke 12.39–40, **55**
Luke 12.42-46, **57**
Luke 12.57–59, **21**
Luke 13.6–9, **81**
Luke 13.18–19, **7**
Luke 13.20–21, **31**
Luke 13.24–30, **83**
Luke 14.7–11, **85**
Luke 14.16–24, **49**
Luke 14.28–33, **87**
Luke 15.3–7, **39**
Luke 15.8–10, **89**
Luke 15.11–32, **91**
Luke 16.1–8, **95**
Luke 16.19–31, **97**
Luke 17.7—10, **101**
Luke 18.1–8, **103**
Luke 18.9–14, **105**
Luke 19.12–27, **64**
Luke 20.9–18, **10**
Luke 21.29–33, **14**
Luke 23.36, **117**

Mark 4.1–9, **1**
Mark 4.26–29, **5**
Mark 4.30–32, **7**
Mark 12.1–11, **9**
Mark 13.28–37, **13**

Mark 13.33–37, **17**
Mark 15.41, **117**
Mark 16, **117**

Matthew 2, **116**
Matthew 5.1-11, **111**
Matthew 5.25–26, **21**
Matthew 5.27, **116**
Matthew 5.31, **116**
Matthew 7.24–27, **23**
Matthew 11.16–19, **25**
Matthew 12.43–45, **27**
Matthew 13.1–9, 18–23, **2**
Matthew 13.24–30, **29**
Matthew 13.31–32, **7**
Matthew 13.33, **31**
Matthew 13.44, **33**
Matthew 13.45, **35**
Matthew 13.47–50, **37**

Matthew 15.21, **117**
Matthew 18.12–14, **39**
Matthew 18.23–35, **41**
Matthew 20.1–16, **43**
Matthew 21.28–32, **47**
Matthew 21.33–44, **9**
Matthew 22.1–11, **49**
Matthew 22.11–14, **53**
Matthew 24.32–39, **13**
Matthew 24.43–44, **55**
Matthew 24.45–51, **57**
Matthew 25.1–13, **61**
Matthew 25.14–30, **63**
Matthew 25.31–46, **67**
Matthew 27.55, **117**
Matthew 28, **117**

II Samuel 12.1-7, **v**

www.ingramcontent.com/pod-product-compliance
Lightning Source LLC
Chambersburg PA
CBHW020749230426
43665CB00009B/546